Toward Interfaith Harmony

Why People Believe
Or Not,
And Where Differences
Take Us Next

Toward Interfaith Harmony

Why People Believe
Or Not,
And Where Differences
Take Us Next

Marshall L. Shearer, MD

Fresh Ink Group
Guntersville

Toward Interfaith Harmony:
Why People Believe or Not,
And Where Differences Take Us Next

Fresh Ink Group
An Imprint of:
The Fresh Ink Group, LLC
Box 931
Guntersville, AL 35976
Email: info@FreshInkGroup.com
FreshInkGroup.com

Edition 1.0   2017

Book design by Ann Stewart / FIG

Cover by Stephen Geez / FIG

Cover art by Anik / FIG

All biblical quotations reference
Holy Bible, New International Version
Copyright 1973, 1978, 1984
International Bible Society

BISAC Subject Headings:
REL017000 RELIGION / Comparative Religion
REL075000 RELIGION / Psychology of Religion
SOC039000 SOCIAL SCIENCE / Sociology of Religion

Library of Congress Control Number: 2017917108

Hardcover ISBN-13: 978-1-936442-61-4
Paper-cover ISBN-13: 978-1-936442-60-7
Ebook ISBN-13: 978-1-936442-62-1

To everyone who strives
for harmony among the religions
within their minds
or in the world

Table of Contents

Introduction

The Goal

My goal in writing this book is to promote interfaith understanding, respect, and acceptance; and to enhance brotherhood and sisterhood, thereby bringing the people of other religions inside these circles of concern. Some people are only concerned for themselves; or for their families, their country, or those who are members of the same religion; or for all the people of the world. These circles may be viewed as concentric circles, one inside another. As one's circle of understanding and concern for others expands, the prospects for world peace grow.

The Approaches

The first approach is to consider the many often-poignant ways the major religions of the world are quite similar. Others have recognized the similarities, e.g.: the establishment in 1893 of the Parliament of the World's Religions[1]; the 1948 issuance by the United Nations of *Universal Declaration of Human Rights*[2]; and the issuance of *Toward a Global Ethic* by the 1993 Chicago Parliament of the World's Religions.[3]

I will examine the gross similarities of religion, not those concepts or aspects that make any particular religion unique, or that confer its identity. Some religions have more detailed and perhaps more beautiful levels of understanding than what we will be discussing. Christianity, for example, separates its concept of love into agape and eros. This distinction is very meaningful to many Christians, but it is at a level of detail that is not common across religions. When differences are encountered it will be meaningful to note which aspects of religions are different.

To aid in these comparisons and not to be overwhelmed by the sheer volume of facts, the distinctions among feelings, thoughts, and actions will be used. A similar approach was used by Friedrich Schleiermacher in 1799 in his book *On Religion: Discourses Addressed to the Cultured Critic*,[4] and by Rudolf Otto, who did an extensive study comparing religious emotions across the religions of five continents. He published his findings in 1917 in *The Idea of the Holy*.[5] Our feelings, thoughts, and actions shape, and to a large extent are shaped by, our religions.

Feelings: The overarching religious feeling is love: love of the Divine, and love of fellow humans. These are the emotions of reverence, piety, wonder, and awe.

They include feelings of deep dependency and the sense of the presence of "another," a sense of "otherness." The triggers for these feelings vary greatly from one religion to another, and even among different members in the same religious traditions.

Thoughts: The largest differences among the religions are in the realms of thought and in rituals, i.e.: the stories, histories, myths, creeds, and doctrines. However, thought has led to a deliberate core of ethics that is very similar among the world's religions.[6] Representatives of every major religion were signatories to "The Declaration of the Parliament of World Religions on Global Ethics" in Chicago in 1993. Thoughts lead to creating religious organizations.

Every organization has two principles: to fulfill its mission, and to maintain and perpetuate the organization. This distinction can be seen in the Judeo-Christian Ten Commandments. The first four commandments concern one's relationship with God. They relate to the perpetuation of the religion. The next six deal with their mission. They are concerned with issues of social justice among people.[7] The ways in which various religions deal with their perpetuation differ widely, whereas the ideals of religions' missions are very similar.

Actions: Prescriptions for religions' actions are taken from their sacred scriptures. Similarities are documented in regard to The Golden Rule, the giving of alms, the admonishments to forgive fellow humans, and the prescriptions for social justice. They also include prescribed—or customary—acts of worship.

The second approach is to point out many of the aspects of human nature that further the human search for religious meaning. Rudolf Otto points out that the word that is translated as "holy" in several languages comes from the word meaning "other," as opposed to the self.

Humans have always been spiritual, and they have always used religion to understand and express their spirituality. There is something intrinsic in human nature that draws people toward religious concepts and phenomena. Part of this is the need to relate to something greater than the self. Part is the phenomena often experienced when an individual focuses his/her full attention on a religious subject and maintains that focus for an extended period. This is one way a mystical experience is induced. This response appears to be built into the neurophysiology of the brain.[8]

It is the business of religions to address the existential questions: "Where did we come from?" or "Where were we before we were born?" "What is the purpose of life?" or "How should I live my life?" and "What happens to us after we die?" "Is there individual existence after death?"

There are several other significant mental mechanisms that the reader needs to be aware of:

1. **Modalities intersect.** There is a 3-way intersection among feelings, thoughts, and actions, i.e.: the trigger may arise in any of the modalities, and spread to one or the other two. Some people develop the habit that a particular emotion may trigger a different one, e.g.: a hurt may be experienced as anger, bypassing even the awareness of the hurt feeling.

2. **People develop habits.** A person may develop a habit for a particular trigger for any one of these modalities, and one modality can trigger another modality.

3. **Modalities are contagious.** Emotions are especially contagious. Anger, fear, laughter, and sexual arousal can bounce between two or more people to reach a fever pitch.

4. **People share.** They need to verbally share experiences that are emotionally important. Often this need is manifest in the verbal recounting of the story after the action is over. This tends to foster friendships, confidants, and communities.

The third approach is to cite sacred scriptures and to use historical examples to illustrate many of the points.

Shifting Religious Concepts

The next chapters deal with how religions sometimes go awry. Most prominent is the reality that people don't necessarily live up to their ideals. We tend to be idealistic when writing guidelines for our intentions, but don't always follow them. One example is the United States' "Declaration of Independence": "… We hold these truths to be self-evident: that all men are created equal…" Yet a number of the signers owned slaves. Also, people commonly do not live up to the New Year's resolutions they make. Other ways people and religions may "get off the track" occur when society changes so much that religious concepts or symbols no longer represent the Infinite. One of the numerous examples Paul Tillich gives is the word "sin." Tillich states that a common reaction to the word "sin" is to think "I have not sinned." However, if the sermon is on estrangement from God, most everyone can identify with the concept.

When significant change occurs, the symbols and concept(s) may become meaningless. Individuals and societies may feel empty. The world itself may no longer hold meaning for them. Traditionally, the prophets, mystics, and poets have pointed out religion's deficiencies. I will describe many of the ways religions deal with losing the meaningfulness of their concepts and symbols.

People want a whole cosmological system, and they are capable of gross distortions even of their own goals to achieve it. Some can be quite troublesome. Some groups or societies may fear losing their religion. This can lead to extreme or radical fundamentalism, attacking whomever or whatever they believe threatens their religious values. The inquisitions are good examples.

I also consider the numerous ways humans have sent and received messages to and from the supernatural.

The Birth of Ethical Religions

Perhaps the most drastic changes in religions occurred in what has been called the Axial Age, which included the birth of ethics and social justice throughout the civilized world. It was centered in the 6th and 5th centuries BCE. Many religions shifted from sacrifices and burnt offerings to an emphasis on human relationships. In Judaism, this shift occurs in the time of Isaiah and Jeremiah[9], and is also described in other books of the *Bible*.[10] In Hinduism, the Upanishads were written. Buddhism, Confucianism, and Zoroastrianism were founded.

Religions are often used during war to inflame passions, enhance conflict, and marshal support for leaders. Some governments have used religion as a unifying theme in their domains. Some leaders have used force, torture, and murder to compel people's compliance with a religion's practices. Mohammad said, "Let there be no coercion in matters of religion."[11] Aside from the feeling that one's religion is threatened, nothing in religion per se causes war. No religion teaches that war is an ideal to which all should aspire. Many countries have several dominant religions that peacefully co-exist.

During the Axial Age, Confucianism arose to specify the proper relationships between people of different social stations. Buddha, known as the Compassionate One, lived during this time. In Persia, Zoroastrianism presented life as a struggle between good and evil. The movement spread to Greece in the time of Socrates. The fate and the whims of gods and goddesses were replaced by a sense of right and wrong. Humans now were to have a conscience. They were to treat fellow humans with fairness and respect. Although humility became essential, that does not contradict the importance of self-esteem.[12]

Toward Interfaith Harmony also includes examples of how some religious communities meet the needs of their members and, in doing so, thrive. The book concludes by stressing the universal values of social justice, respect, forgiveness, charity, and love of others. It recognizes and honors diversity in local or ethnic beliefs and practices. This recognition should lead to genuine acceptance—not just tolerance—of others and other religions. Thomas Jefferson, arguing for laws of religious toleration in the Colony of Virginia, said, "It does me no harm for my neighbor to say there are twenty gods or no god. It neither picks my pocket nor breaks my leg."

The world needs multiple religions. People are often at different points in their religious development. No one is capable of understanding all the manifestations and facets of the Infinite.

The early Christian judgments about other religions were dominated by the concept of the ever-present Logos. Jesus continued the trend to universalism by repeatedly violating Jewish ritual laws. A religion will be lasting to the extent it breaks with its own narrowness to become universal.

Schleiemacher says the purpose of all religions is to enhance the growth of love. Love overcomes separateness and brings us into communion with the Ultimate, the God of Justice, the admonition for compassion, the God of Love, and the God of Mercy. These are one and the same.

As you read this book, consider this important question: How big is your circle of love?

NOTES FOR INTRODUCTION

Intro.1   Parliament of the World's Religions, Chicago, 1893, See www.inplain-site.org/html/parliament_world_religions.html

Intro.2   *Universal Declaration of Human Rights, The New Encyclopaedia Britannica*, 15ᵗʰ Ed, Vol 7, Encyclopaedia Britannica, Inc., 1990, p. 163-4

Intro.3   Parliament of the World's Religions, Chicago, 1993. www.inplainsite.org/html/parliament_world_religions.html

Intro.4   Schleiermacher, Friedrich: *On Religion: Addresses in Response to its Cultured Critics*, Tice, Terrence N., trans., Knox Press, Richmond, VA, 1969

Intro.5   Otto, Rudolf: *The Idea of the Holy*, Galaxy Book, NYC, 1958

Intro.6   See Chapter Four, "Global Ethics"

Intro.7   *Bible*: Exodus 20

Intro.8   See Chapter Seven

Intro.9   *Bible*: Isaiah 1:10-26 & Jeremiah 22:13-17

Intro.10   *Bible*: Hosea, Amos, & Micah

Intro.11   *Qur'an*: "The House of Imran," "Mutual Fraud," Arberry, A.J., trans., MacMillan Pub Co., New York, 1955

Intro.12   See Chapter Eleven, "Self-love," " Self-esteem"

CHAPTER ONE

Mental Mechanisms

The mental mechanisms that result in harmony or dissonance in an individual's world view are the same regardless of religion. Many are easy to recognize. Understanding how people think is an important step toward understanding how they think about religion.

The human mind is constantly trying to establish order, to harmonize and integrate all its facets into a coherent whole. Because such synthesis is usually successful, any lack of integration is especially noticeable. If the integration is incomplete or faulty, dissonance and stress may result. A good example was given by Mark Twain in *Tom Sawyer:*

> *As a boy takes a shortcut home through the graveyard at night, he has an eerie feeling and grows scared. He reminds himself that he doesn't believe in ghosts or spirits, that there are no such things! These thoughts do not change his feelings, so he tries whistling a happy tune and acting nonchalant. His feelings, thoughts, and actions are all at variance, each with the other two. Such dissonance is stressful, and in a short time his feeling of fear overcomes both his reasoning thought and the forced casualness of his actions. He thinks, This is stupid; why am I doing this? He breaks into a headlong dash toward home. The act of running adds to and reinforces his fear, but all three of his modalities—his thoughts, feelings, and actions—are now in harmony.[1]*

Actions of bravery and heroism result from a thought, the decision to act for the benefit of another despite danger and the feelings of fear and stress. In every aspect of life, one's values, notably in their role as thoughts, become part of self-identity. At all levels of thought, what we call our *values* are judgments (conscious and unconscious) of what we consider important, both by priority and degree. At the perceptual level, we have millions of such judgments, some of which get organized into concepts and become thoughts. Factual discriminations may accompany and interact with these value judgments. Failure to live up to one's values can create even greater stress and even result in guilt or self-loathing.

Integration Difficulties

The more important an issue is to the individual, the greater the need to integrate, and the greater the stress arising from lack of integration. Often, a person in historical or fictional accounts is portrayed as being conflicted between some strong desire and "doing the right thing." This conflict may be quite real or only imagined. It may be frivolous, misperceived, or created and/or maintained for some unknown reason. Sometimes reality precludes full integration, as in a desire to stay with one's family versus a duty to join the armed forces. When reality-based conflicts involving particularly important issues remain unresolved, the individual needs to be consciously aware of the impasse. He needs to prioritize his values, then make his choice. For instance, famous WWI soldier Sergeant York reported a deep internal struggle between his value not to kill others and his value of fighting for his country. He spent much time in prayer and contemplation, re-examining his values. Then he consciously chose! Another example is how the attack on Pearl Harbor in December, 1941, changed the ordinary priority of values for any Americans who previously favored isolationism.

Sometimes an impasse may be resolved other ways, such as in obtaining new corrective information. For example, in *Sexual Behavior in the Human Male*[2] Kinsey reported the incidence and frequency of masturbation by age and level of education. This information relieved or reduced feelings of guilt for a large number of men. Some individuals may choose to continue living with an impasse, such as continuing to work at a job they hate and to endure the resultant stress.

Another example of the conflict between desire (feeling) and thought can be found in Jesus' reported prayer in Gethsemane.

> "My Father, if it is possible, let this cup pass from me; yet not what
> I want but what you want."[3]

Muslims resolve these conflicts by the doctrine of surrendering to the will of Allah.

With or without the recognition of an impasse, the mind will continue efforts at integration, including during sleep. For Sergeant York, working out his values and making a clear conscious choice allowed him to be effective in combat. Some first-time combatants with similar unresolved conflicts never fire their rifles. Sometimes the pressure to integrate results in major vacillations and inconsistencies in both thought and action. Sometimes the pressure to integrate is so great that the individual forces or falsifies the synthesis. Unconscious forcing may involve creating a new "piece of data." It may involve eliminating one piece of data to allow the other data to fit.

For several reasons, the most common time for these faulty integrations and forced alterations is childhood. At each stage of development, children have a great deal to integrate, which they are attempting only with the level of understanding appropriate to their age. Here is an example of faulty integration by a four-year-old boy.

A boy is told that food he eats goes into his tummy. Later he is eating an orange with his grandmother. On seeing a seed, he asks what it is, then expresses doubt when told an orange tree could grow from that seed if planted. His grandmother pokes the seed into the edge of a flower pot on the table next to her chair. After two or three weeks, a slender green shoot appears. Some months later, his mother delivers her second child. In response to his question, "Where do babies come from?" he is told that they come from a seed that Daddy put in Mother's tummy. With this syllogism, there is only one logical conclusion: "If I eat an orange seed, an orange will grow in my tummy." This fear of orange seeds is then generalized to all seeds.

While the problem with this conclusion is obvious to adults, other conclusions drawn from faulty integration during childhood can persist into adulthood. Irrational fears, unusual beliefs, superstitions, and even some of one's religious thinking can stem from instances of faulty integration at an early age.

Defense Mechanism

When something changes in the emotional realm (feeling), it often activates of a defense mechanism, e.g.: repression or taking the opposite approach, rationalization, compartmentalization, projection, emotional denial, and so forth. If change—alteration—occurs in the realm of thinking, it may involve confabulation, i.e.: the individual is consciously or unconsciously filling in the gaps in data or logic with what is most likely, or what he wants it to be. Confabulations are a function of the mind being a great integrator or synthesizer. Usually, adolescents and adults are aware they have "filled in the gap," just as these individuals can distinguish a dream from something that really happened. However, if the confabulation fits well, in time the individual may come to assume the validity of the confabulation, even forgetting that it was a confabulation. All too often, conclusions are drawn without limiting the circumstances or applicability of the change.

Whatever their cause, mental alterations tend to become all-encompassing principles, assumptions, or even "life scripts" that people live by unconsciously. For example, a parent may repeatedly call his child "stupid" and "worthless."

Since the child believes the parent is always right, and nobody contradicts the message, he may come to believe it as a new life script:

"I'm a bad person. I don't deserve to be happy or to be successful."

Unconscious life scripts are held on to with even greater tenacity than when a person is fully aware of the same values. Conscious personal values are more accessible to a person's mind and, hence, to re-evaluation than what we are calling life scripts. Initially, the "pieces of data" that have led to the conclusion that became a life script were very emotionally charged, and are frequently incorporated into one's thinking, then forgotten or repressed. These highly organized structures of facts and values are not so readily available to consciousness, or for re-evaluation, as they were originally.

Alteration may also occur in the realm of action. These acts are often falsely interpreted as results of "stupidity."

A man attempts to rob a bank with his finger and thumb as a gun, but "forgets" to keep his hand in his pocket. Another interpretation of this act is that he wants to be caught (for an unknown reason). A third interpretation is that his value system would not allow him to rob the bank any more than it would allow him to risk shooting someone by carrying a real gun into the bank.

Another example of action alteration is a man who cheats on his taxes but then cannot enjoy the money he saves due to guilt. We are sometimes totally unaware of such conflicts and "slips" in ourselves. Misspeaking or slips of speech and alterations in action are well documented by Sigmund Freud[4] and by August Aichhorn.[5] They occur in everyone, in some quite frequently.

We pay a price for incorrect synthesis or incomplete integration by losing energy to be creative with the synthesis, as well as suffering the undesirable "side effects" of a faulty or incomplete synthesis. In addition, some ongoing mental energy is required to maintain the defense mechanism or forced integration. We are likely to experience anxiety or other symptoms if the faulty integration begins to come undone. These facts are responsible for the "resistance" seen in psychoanalysis and other therapies.

Feelings, Thoughts, and Actions Defined

Feelings: The word "feeling" is used to refer to the state of mind of an individual, such as happiness, sadness, embarrassment, anxiety, or fear. The word "emotion(s)" refers to more than just the feeling state. It also includes the body's response to the feeling state, such as facial expression, blushing, muscle tension, being wide-eyed, or showing anger or fear. Someone may turn red with anger or pale with fear. Therapists routinely learn from their patients that many feeling states are mixtures of feelings. For example, in feeling hurt (put down), one may also feel powerless, helpless, and /or angry. In this respect, the expression most commonly used by patients is "I feel." "Feel" has two other major uses. It is used to describe internal physical states, such as feeling sleepy, tired, hungry, or nauseated. "Feel" is also used to describe touch and other contact with the environment, e.g.: "I feel cold," "The fabric feels smooth," "I felt the vibrations of the engine through my feet," and "He felt the ground give way under his feet."

The recognition of a feeling becomes a thought.

Thoughts: Thoughts are expressed to the self or others as sentences, even if some parts of a sentence are understood without being expressed. Thus, a sentence is usually defined as a complete thought. The verbal communication of a feeling has become a thought. A woman may become warm, then unbutton her coat without it necessarily becoming a thought. In that instance, she acts automatically without thinking. However, if she focuses attention on the feeling, it becomes a thought. Feelings can be communicated without words, at times without becoming a thought, as two lovers can certainly attest. Thinking about every action rather than being in tune with one's partner and allowing one's feelings to flow directly into actions can destroy some intimacy.

Actions: Actions involve muscles that are typically under voluntary control. Thus, stomach growlings and blushing are not "actions." Speaking, screaming, eye blinking, and breathing are actions, even though they can also occur automatically without thinking. This distinction is consistent with the type of fibers of the muscle involved. *Striated muscle fibers* control voluntary actions. *Smooth muscle fibers* are generally not under voluntary control

There is a three-way relation among feeling, thinking, and acting; each can influence one or both of the other two. Any of these three aspects of mental functioning can influence the physiology of the body, and the body can influence each or all aspects of the mind. They are interactive aspects, not separate faculties. Without detailing all the intricate interconnections, let us consider how feelings, thoughts, and actions operate within the mind-body, including the special functions that can be assigned to religion.

Feelings Discussed

Feelings arise from all that is our past, and are triggered by something current. Feelings are not necessarily logical. Sometimes simple feelings converge to form complex feelings or *affective states* such as moods, and clinical conditions such as anxiety and depression. Feelings may be contradictory to what a person knows. For example, a person may know that he or she is loved, yet *feel* unloved. A person may have multiple feelings, or even mutually contradictory feelings at the same time. This situation is called ambivalence. Contradictory feelings do not cancel each other out as a set of positive and negative numbers do.

Feelings are not under direct voluntary control. A person cannot change a feeling by saying, "I am not going to feel sad or embarrassed any longer; instead, I am going to feel happy and free of embarrassment," and throw some mental switch to have the feelings change. However, will power can be used to direct thoughts, and in this way feelings can be indirectly changed. Focusing thoughts on happy times will reduce unhappy or disturbing feelings. Some people habitually use fantasies to replace unwanted feelings. How feelings can change with a shift in thought was brought home to me at my father's funeral:

> *My father died unexpectedly. My grief was heavy. At that time my mother was past-president of the Southern Baptist Women's Missionary Union for the state of South Carolina. I was concerned about how my mother was holding up through memorial services held in two states with relatives and friends crying on her shoulder, and she on theirs, hour after hour. It took me several minutes each time to make a judgment about whether she was becoming overwhelmed with her grief and the contagion of the emotionally expressed grief and sympathy of others, and whether I needed to intervene to give her a brief respite. I was surprised that during those times of evaluation my own feelings of grief, which had been so heavy, disappeared. My grief returned as soon as I had concluded that my mother didn't need me to intervene.*

Feelings may be suppressed or repressed. *Repression* is unconscious, not an intentional act. *Suppression* is conscious and intentional, such as diverting one's attention to other thoughts.

Feelings trigger responses. A feeling or an emotion arises at a particular time as the result of a stimulus or trigger. The trigger may be a perception, an interaction, or a realization, even one that resulted from synthesis. Receiving credible news that a loved one has died unexpectedly may trigger grief and sadness. A dispute might trigger resentment, hurt, and anger. Watching a hail storm knock all the blossoms from his fruit trees will likely trigger a farmer's sadness and perhaps worry about his income. Watching offspring perform well may trigger a parent's pride and satisfaction. Although most triggers are culturally determined and therefore variable, those examples are close to universal.

One feeling can also trigger another. Many men shift from a psychological hurt to anger so rapidly that they do not experience the feeling of being hurt. They only register the insult intellectually—in thought. Feelings and emotions do vary in intensity, depending on the type of trigger, the meaning to the individual, and the individual's make-up—"cold reactor" or "hot reactor." Culture is also a major determining factor of intensity.

Feelings and emotions also have a response component, which may include dismissing the feeling, contemplating it, or taking action. Each individual has a repertoire of responses for each emotion. These are largely influenced by culture. Generally speaking, the larger the response repertoire an individual has for each emotion, the more mature the individual.

Feelings vary in intensity. The intensity of any emotion can be reduced significantly by thought as critical judgment. I temporarily reduced my feeling of grief over my father's death by concentrating on the mental status of my mother. Another example is a studio musician offered a chance to perform before an audience. If he becomes preoccupied with worries about hitting a wrong note, his thoughts and resulting anxiety can interfere with him feeling the music in a way that connects with listeners.

The more someone dwells on the trigger of a feeling, the more detail is recalled or imagined, the more intense the feeling becomes and the more intense the urge to act follows it. Dwelling on feelings easily moves to dwelling on thoughts, including fantasy and daydreaming and considering possible actions. Anger can be reduced by thinking of the second or third level of another's motivation, e.g.: "Why would she say that? And why now? I thought we were both feeling close," rather than concentrating on the feeling of hurt it caused.

Emotions are contagious. All emotions are as contagious as the common cold. However, not everyone who comes in contact with another person who has a strong feeling develops that feeling any more than everyone who comes in contact with a person who has a bad cold will develop the cold. The greater the intensity in expressing an emotion, the greater the likelihood of contagion. In some circumstances, the contagion builds between two or more people. Before the days of modern medicine, a standard technique of the midwife was to send the anxious husband off to boil water. This reduced the man's tension and reduced the contagious effect of his anxiety on his wife and those helping her. Feelings of arousal can bounce between two lovers with ever-increasing intensity. Hurt and anger can build between people to the point that they are expressed in physical assault. Cursing may relieve the need for further actions, but if the cursing is directed at another, it may incite action in the other person. Joy, pleasant excitement, and humor are just as contagious as any other emotional states.

Feelings are distinctly our own. However, since we cannot directly, willfully control our feelings, we are not responsible for their immediate occurrence. Nonetheless, we are totally accountable for what we choose to focus our thoughts on. We are also responsible for how we choose to act on the basis of those feelings, including what we do to increase the chances of changing those feelings in the desired direction. Ordinarily, the more a person dwells on the current trigger of a feeling, and the more detail he or she recalls or imagines to fill in the gaps, the more intense a feeling becomes and the greater is the urge to act.

Thoughts Discussed

One of the greatest motivators of human behavior is that drive to satisfy desires. While "wants" often originate from feelings, pursuing the goal of achieving or acquiring them results in conscious thought. If a desired object is perceived as one of a kind, or if someone believes it is beyond his or her means, then the desire may lead to coveting—the thought of acquiring something that belongs to another by immoral and perhaps illegal means, e.g.: theft, adultery, or murder. If these thoughts are not dismissed, they may lead to speculation: "Would it be possible?" and "How might I (or anyone) do it and get away with it?" At first, the individual may consider the question only as an idle mental exercise. The challenge of the question may add impetus to thinking out a plausible scheme. As a plan begins to take shape, he or she identifies the stumbling blocks and focuses on finding solutions to them. The urge to carry out the plan successfully becomes more and more of an ego trip. The greater the challenge, the greater the ego trip.

Perhaps because the force of additional motivating factors was recognized, the Ten Commandments do not stop after "You shall not murder," "You shall not commit adultery," "You shall not steal," and "You shall not bear false witness against your neighbor (commit perjury)." The Ten Commandments end with, "You shall not covet your neighbor's house; you shall not covet your neighbor's wife, or male or female slave, or ox, or donkey, or anything that belongs to your neighbor."[7] In other words, Don't even *think* about it. Some dismiss thoughts that do not fit with their value systems with the words, "Get behind me, Satan." The twentieth-century equivalent, in the words of the pioneer of behavior modification therapy, Joseph Wolpe,[8] is: "Thought(s) stop."

Usually play and fantasy among the young arise from their perception or misperception of adult activities in their lives, or they represent things children dream of doing as adults. Thought of a fantasy or plan may be viewed as trial action to consider the potential outcomes in regard to one's own feelings, the perceptions of others, and the impact of reality. Some fantasies should not be entertained at all: fantasies that would generate guilt or shame, or that would otherwise violate the individual's value system. These thoughts are often called temptations. Consider these guidelines:

1. **Don't continue fantasizing about a theme that generates guilt or shame.** Often the beginning of a fantasy comes up unbidden. Don't continue it if it would generate negative feelings, especially if it came to light; or if it would otherwise violate your value system, regardless of any differences between your current age and your fantasized age.

2. **Re-examine your value system if it is unrealistically strict.** If you find that you are unable to enjoy any strong repeated fantasy, such as that of being really successful or enjoying an intimate relationship, without violating one of your ideals or principles, then you probably need to re-examine your value system or seek professional help.

Observance of these admonitions by teenagers regarding their fantasies would prevent a number of sexual problems in their adult lives. Circumstances permitting, adults do not have to just "live with" the results. The problems may be ameliorated or eliminated by active reflection, experience, or therapy.

Actions Discussed

The more intense the feeling or the more important an issue, the greater the psychological need to integrate. By using muscles that are usually under voluntary control, *striated muscle*, action usually reduces anxiety. "Somebody do something!"

Faced with a terminal illness, an individual's need to do something, to try almost anything after medicine has nothing more to offer except palliative treatment, is very strong. This need for action may contribute to the unwary individual or family becoming victims of con artists.

A scream is an action, even if no words are in the scream. A scream may be used to attract attention or to appeal for help, or it may simply be the action component of fright in order to reduce tension. Running, exercising, slamming, or engaging in a sport may discharge tension, if only temporarily.

When thoughts and feelings are strong but unconscious, the person is likely to "act out," which is an effort to establish harmony as well as to meet other emotional goals. However, the relief of tension is only temporary. The act is likely to be repeated when the individual experiences similar triggers. Since that behavior gave some relief in the past, it is used again and again. The act may become habit, and the habit usually grows in intensity and frequency. Assaultive behavior is an example. It may be *repeated* in a succession of relationships. The vicious cycles may stop only when the individual consciously recognizes all the feelings and thoughts that are the current triggers, as well as thoughts and feelings from the past. Only then will the individual be in a position to understand and to re-synthesize his or her troublesome life experiences sufficiently to achieve harmony and to relieve the need to act out. In professional circles, this process is usually called psychoanalysis or psychoanalytically oriented psychotherapy. When successful, it enables a re-integration more in keeping with reality, resulting in greater inner harmony.

People and animals tend to be creatures of habit. They develop habits of feeling, of interpretation of events, and of expressing emotions by words and other actions. These emotional habits may be seen in repeated use of the same set of "swear words" if a person curses. The level of frustration that is tolerable prior to an "explosion" is usually characteristic in each given person. *Optimistic* and *pessimistic* are adjectives used to describe a person's usual interpretation of events. One therapy patient said, "When people are nice to me, I become angry because I think they are being devious and manipulative." In accordance with the principles of conditioning, as a person's feeling, thinking, and acting become associated with each other; they become mutually reinforcing, and they tend to become habitual.

Humans are social animals. We need others, not just for mates and families, but also for buddies, for confidants. We need mutual support and networks of friends. People need to share. The process of describing a feeling and its thought and action triggers is often called *sharing*. Sharing of this type may engender sympathy for sadness and loss, empathy for hardship, good fellowship for pleasant emotions. Any of these is a step toward community-building. Sympathy, empathy, and good relationships contain an element of identification between or among participants. Concentrating on positive thoughts adds to happiness, whether planning and anticipating or reminiscing about happy times. Sharing may involve joining group activities of thinking, such as directed meditations or just listening. It may involve group activities of action such as singing or kneeling to pray. The sharing of thoughts and actions among a group of religious worshipers is intended to engender feelings of reverence and caring and community.

Archbishop Desmond Tutu offers a good example of value in sharing. In order to be granted amnesty, perpetrators who testified before the Truth and Reconciliation Commission had to give full and complete accounts of what they had done. They had to acknowledge responsibility and guilt. Victims also testified. After the hearings, many from both groups stated that they found relief, experiencing catharsis and healing just through the process of telling and hearing their experiences.[9]

What Is Cultural and What Is Universal?

Triggers for a feeling, what that feeling means to the individual, and how he or she responds to the feeling vary widely, not only across cultures, but even within a family. Feelings of reverence are usually cultural. However, there is a core of each feeling state or emotion that is universal. This is true for all religious feelings. People tend to regard these feeling states as desirable, which largely accounts for the ubiquitous appeal of religion and spirituality. It also accounts for the fact that until the 20th century every society had some form of religion.

These same general principles presented for feelings, thinking, and acting in general are also applicable in the area of religion.

NOTES FOR CHAPTER ONE

1.1   Twain, Mark: *The Adventures of Tom Sawyer*, American Publishing Company, 1876

1.2   Kinsey, Alfred; Pomroy, Wardell; and Martin, Clyde: *Sexual Behavior in the Human Male*, W.B. Saunders Co., Philadelphia, 1948

1.3   *Bible*: Matthew 26:39

1.4   Freud, Sigmund: *Psychopathology of Everyday Life*, Tyson, Alan, trans., W.W. Norton Co., NY, 1960

1.5   Aichhorn, August: *Wayward Youth*, Meridian Books, 1935

1.6   *Encyclopaedia Britannica*, 15th Ed, Vol 7, Encyclopaedia Britannica, Inc., p. 285

1.7   *Bible*: Exodus 20

1.8   Wolpe, Joseph, MD: *The Practice of Behavior Therapy*, "Thought-Stopping," Pergamon Press, NYC, 1969, p. 110, 224

1.9   Tutu, Archbishop Desmond: *No Future Without Forgiveness*, Image Doubleday, NYC, 1999, p. 51-55 & 165

CHAPTER TWO

Religious Feelings

Love

Love is the overarching emotion of all religions—love of God and love of fellow humans. Love begins as a feeling. It matures into much more, but remains mainly an emotion. In Hinduism, the highest ideal of humankind, namely to spread the message of love and brotherhood among all people, is called *Arya-Dharma*.[1] Love in its broadest sense encircles all humankind.

Religious feelings also include reverence and compassion. Reverence is toward God, worship observances, and religious rituals. Compassion and empathy are toward all who are inside the individual's circle of concern (love)—even toward all the world. This division of reverence toward God (or the Divine) and compassion toward fellow people is the major division that is found in all religions. Mercy is also a religious feeling, with different forks: mercy expected from God, and mercy granted toward others. Both the Old and New Testament support this.

One of the main functions of worship is to engender feelings of closeness to God and to fellow worshipers, perhaps extending to everyone. People also feel close to God when thinking of sacred concepts or objects, or when acts of love are expressed or witnessed. During periods of religious persecution, people hide and protect their copies of sacred scriptures because they feel close to God while reading or studying them.

There is a reverence for the divine spark or potential in every human. Recognition of this spark leads to the Hindu custom of bowing to the spark others. In Christian terms, this sense of love is *agape*. It is love whether or not the individual deserves to be loved. That is the Christian teaching of God's love for each person. Love from one person to another is recognition of this divinity. Love is also found in humble self-love, whether or not the individual feels or believes that he/she deserves it.[2]

The Dalai Lama from Tibet thus asserts: "Every major religion of the world has similar ideas of love, the same goal of benefiting humanity through spiritual practice, and the same effect of making their followers into better human beings."[3]

The stated goal of all religions is love. The purpose of religion is to enhance the growth of love. "All growth toward perfection in religion is simply a progressive purification of love."[4]

At the non-personal level, love is replaced by social justice.

Religions also generate feelings of hope and security, for the individual and for the culture, which counter feelings of fear, loneliness, hopelessness, insecurity, and inadequacy when not understanding.

Religious Feelings Are at the Core of Authentic Religion

In 1799 Friedrich Schleiermacher was a young German philosopher, pastor, and theologian who published the book *On Religion: Addresses in Response to its Cultured Critics*. Since then, he has been regarded as the father of modern theology and founder of the modern study of religion. In *On Religion* he stated that feeling has a crucial stimulating, mediating, and expressive role to play in all human life, particularly in relation to thinking and acting. There is no such thing as "mere feeling." Feelings of love always generate thoughts of the loved object and a strong need to be close to that which is loved, be it God, humans, or a romantic lover. Love overcomes separateness. Love also contains a motivation to secure justice for the loved, whether this be for an individual or for the whole city or society. Schleiemacher saw religious feelings as the very core of authentic religion, at any and all stages of its development.

He emphasized that the inner core of religion lies in a certain feeling and in an inner sense of the wholeness that accompanies it. He called it "the feeling of dependence on the infinite." This feeling can rise to the highest level of consciousness, and to feelings of absolute, unqualified dependence. It is always on this internal basis that religion develops and grows; it does not remain static. Religion is also experienced through community, gaining impetus for each person through others and reciprocally sustaining that influence. This whole process of fulfilling all the aspects of religion for the individual, Schleiermacher called "piety." Piety is the highest end human beings can attain. It cannot be achieved by simply deciding to be pious. It is a process that must arise from within and be recognized by the individual as one's own, beyond any dispute.[5]

Schleiemacher's work was validated by another pioneering German theologian, Rudolf Otto, who republished the 1799 book in 1899. He followed this in 1904 with his own work, *Religion and Naturalism*[6] (translated by Terry Tice), which reported the results of his study of the logical or rational thoughts on religion.

Otto's second book, *The Idea of the Holy*,[7] was the result of his realization that adherents of Christianity often do not recognize the profound impact that feeling Holy makes on people, or that those aspects of religion are non-rational. He also realized, as Schleiermacher had, that since all ideas and concepts are communicated by words, most people conclude that those ideas must be presented as logical and rational. This conclusion further results in the tendency to neglect the grounding of these ideas in feeling—in what is often non-rational.

Otto began his study of religious feelings in 1910. He visited with religious people in North Africa, Egypt, Palestine, India, China, Japan, and the United States. He noted that some primitive tribes often recognize a remote, unapproachable high God who is above or beyond their rituals and ordinary thinking.[8] He was impressed by the marked similarity of the underlying feeling state. He separated those elements that are ethnic or culture-bound, such as ethics and morals, from the feeling state. He arrived at a description of a pure feeling state, the lowest common denominator that seemed to be as applicable to primitive people as to sophisticated priests. By "feeling," he meant more than a mere emotion. It is also the recognition of something in the objective situation awaiting discovery and acknowledgement.[9] Like Schleiermacher before him, Otto considered only the inner feeling aspect of this basic mental state, which he termed the sense of the Holy, the "sacred," or that which transcends merely rational thought and rational action. This is called the *numen* or a *numinous state*. In support of this approach he pointed out that words translated as "holy" or "sacred" in Latin, Greek, Semitic, and other ancient languages are devoid of ethical connotations.[10] The numinous state includes a sense of and recognition of the sublime; and with it there is a turning of attention from the self toward others, a self-forgetfulness.

With minimal intensity these feelings may be experienced as weird, uncanny, or eerie. There is a sense of another's presence,[11] of awe and wonder and fascination with its power, with the majesty and mystery of its otherworldliness, and with its energy and sense of urgency. Otto cited the example of Moses facing the burning bush and holding a conversation with God.[12]

Sense of Holy

Ancient people experienced the holy state in several situations: energy, orderliness, vastness, and regeneration. All of these forms can be identified by contemplating the sky. The sun, moon, and stars move in a cyclical, orderly manner. The sky is the home of the sun, which gives warmth, and of the storm with its lightning and thunder's immense energy. It is little wonder that the most potent god of many peoples has been a thrower of the thunderbolts, such as Zeus, Jupiter, and Odin. The sun dies each night and is reborn each morning. The moon dies and is reborn every month. Many star constellations die each year and are reborn the next. The sky appears unaffected by humans. Regeneration has also been considered Holy. Trees regrow their leaves. Oak trees were held to be sacred by the Druids. Vegetation regenerates each spring. The stag regrows his antlers. The snake regrows his skin. Recognition of these facts can be taken as symbolic of conquering death by anthropocentric-based religious thinkers. All of these symbols, as well as others generate feelings of delight, wonder, awe, and perhaps apprehension—if not fear—are the essence of worship.[13]

The numinous state was likely recognized by the builders of gigantic stone edifices such as Stonehenge or the pyramids of Egypt. Similar intent was expressed in the building of cathedrals, which emphasize the comparative grandeur of God and the smallness of humans. Such monuments are a way to "store up" numen in their solid presence for some people, and to point beyond the structure to that which is transcendent for others.

The numinous feeling state is the feeling that also accompanies the recognition of *the sublime*, regardless of the form or state of the object. It includes purely natural features of the landscape from mountains to waterfalls, even an unusual grove of trees. It also includes natural features that humans have enhanced such as "The Cathedral" in Muir National Forest in California. Other examples include the prehistoric cave paintings of Trois Freres, France, for which the painters took advantage of various bulges in the walls, and the Shinto gardens of Japan. The sublime may also be found in artistic paintings and dance.[14, 15]

Religious Sense of Dependency

As the wonder and majesty of God is experienced more clearly, it may create a sense of smallness and dependency in comparison to the majesty of the Infinite, the Ultimate. This sense of the greatness of God, or "The Other," may be so overwhelming as to result in a sense of loss of identity, and perhaps a sense of horror and dread combined with continuing allure.[16] With mystics these emotions are often referred to as "the dark night of the soul." Otto stated that feelings of the numinous may also occur with encounters that are presumed demonic, as well as holy, and that the West has never had a mysticism of horror as existed for both the Hindus and Buddhists of India. He cited Chapter 11 of *Bhagavad-Gita*.[17] He held that the feeling of dependency is a response to one's awareness of the presence of the Holy, which is felt as objective and outside the self. The numinous feeling state was essentially the same across all the cultures he investigated.[19] Further, from his examination of sacred scripture throughout history, he concluded that humans have been aware of the Holy—a priori—in all cultures of the world and throughout time.

Holy: A Separation from the Self

The Hebrew word *kaddosh*, which is translated "holy," means "otherness"—a radical separation from the self. Otto stated that as the sense of others increases, the sense of self decreases. Religious awareness is a potential feeling in everyone, but it is not always present. It must be recognized and engendered.

Both Schleiermacher and Otto recognized that after the founding of a religion there was a tendency for subsequent generations of religious leaders to focus predominately on their own ethnic group, even if that differed ethnically from the founder's. This had a tendency to either broaden or narrow the scope of the insights. Christianity is a good example. Although Jesus and his disciples were Jews, Christianity quickly moved to the gentiles, and to the Greek and Roman worlds.

Feeling and Reason

Neither Otto nor Schleiermacher would shut off either reason or morals from religion. In the Translator's Preface to Otto's book, his friend John Harvey was careful to point out that Otto did value the moral and rational aspects of religion as well as the non-rational, and that he referred to them as the warp and woof of the fabric of religion. Neither can exist without the other.[20] Harvey stated: "This double note was sounded long ago by Pascal in his *Pensees*: 'If one subjects everything to reason, our religion will lose its mystery and its supernatural character. If one offends the principles of reason, our religion will become absurd and ridiculous…. These are two equally dangerous extremes, to shut reason out and to let nothing else in.'" These two opposites are held together in a creative tension.

Other Religious Feelings

There are other affective states that are especially applicable to religious life. Two are hope and security—as opposed to their opposites: fear, loneliness, hopelessness, insecurity, and lack of understanding. Hope and security serve as intermediate experiences and goals that religion provides individuals or a people. The other affective states are outgrowths of love: compassion and feeling good for having done "the right thing," a reinforcing and confirming feeling, one that is generated by living up to one's religious ideals in thoughts and in actions—in other words, *harmony*. Schleiermacher's analysis opens the way for numerous other feelings and dispositions that can contribute to harmony or work against it, though the basic feeling of wholesome relatedness to the Divine ever remains primary.

NOTES FOR CHAPTER TWO

2.1 Monroe, Charles: *World Religions, An Introduction*, Prometheus Books, Amherst, New York, 1995, p. 83

2.2 See Chapter Eleven, "Self-love," " Self-esteem"

2.3 Moses, Jeffrey, cited by: *Oneness, Great Principles Shared by All Religions*, Fawcett Columbine, 1989

2.4 Schleiermacher, Friedrich: *On Religion: Addresses in Response to its Cultured Critics*, Tice, Terrence N., trans., Knox Press, Richmond, VA, 1969, p. 167

2.5 Schleiermacher: p. 93

2.6 Otto, Rudolf: *Religion and Naturalism*, Tice, Terrance, trans., A Galaxy Book, NYC, 1904

2.7 Otto, Rudolf: *The Idea of the Holy*, A Galaxy Book, Oxford University Press, New York, 1958

2.8 Otto: p. 129

2.9 Otto: p. xvii

2.10 Otto: p. 5

2.11 Otto: p. 9-11

2.12 *Bible*: Exodus 3

2.13 Armstrong, Karen: *A Short History of Myth*, Conongate, New York City, 2005, p. 19

2.14 Otto: p. 65

2.15 Harpur, James: *The Atlas of Sacred Places, Meeting Points of Heaven and Earth*, Henry Holt & Co, NYC, 1994

2.16 Otto: Chapter 4

2.17 Otto: p. 105

2.18 Schleiermacher: p. 93 & Note 7

2.19 Otto: p. x

2.20 Otto: p. xvii

CHAPTER THREE

Religious Thought

For God so loved the world that he gave his only begotten son that whoever believes in Him should not perish, but have eternal life. . . . He who believes in Him is not condemned; he who does not believe in Him is condemned already, because he has not believed in the name of the only son of God. (*Bible*: John 3:16-18)

Belief is thought. In this *Bible* passage it is more than a thought. Just as one modality (feeling, thought, action) can spread to another or both others, this thought is meant to evoke a feeling and result in action. The feeling of truth here is often very deep. In Roman times, some people chose to die rather than deny their Christian beliefs. That choice proves that thought/belief has spread to action. The major world religions are all intellectual (thought) traditions and critical reasoning. Christian theology, based on the *Bible* as its major source, is a tradition of critical reasoning about Christian doctrine, including the question of what should be taught about Jesus Christ.

Religious Thought includes all thoughts about the Divine, or God. Religious thought also includes the name of the Divine or deities, and knowledge of the "proper way" to communicate with the Divine by prayer, ritual, sacrifice, liturgy, mandala, and religious magic. It includes the sacred stories, legends, scriptures, other religious writings, and all myths about the world and the Divine. It includes the history of the religion, and the humans who originated the writings, as well as those who were characters in the writing. It is found in the content of hymns, songs, creeds, doctrines, practicable values, and ideals or principles. It encompasses the standards for religious thoughts and actions. These may be prohibitions ("You shall not bare false witness against your neighbor," *Bible*: Exodus 20:16), prescriptions for thoughts ("Think about these things," *Bible*: Philippians 4:8), or actions (e.g.: the giving of alms). Systems of morality and ethics are part of religious thought. (See Chapter 5) Religious thought also includes the religious interpretations of these. Later religious writings include commentaries on the sacred writings, updated interpretations, and more or less systematic applications or critiques of ideas previously established.

With religious thought the question is, How do we know what we know? How do we know that what we hold to be true is really true? The field attempting to answer these questions is epistemology. Historically, many criteria and systems have been proposed.

Two Approaches to Knowledge

There are two very different approaches to thought and knowledge: *scientific* and *intuitive*. Recognized in religious writings and other disciplines, these distinctions date back to the time of Plato and Aristotle in ancient Greece. They have neurological bases in the brain. The left cerebral cortex is significantly more active when dealing with logic and reason. The right cerebral cortex is more active when dealing with intuition. In common language, this is the basis for the terms *left brain* and *right brain*.[1] In everyday life these two types of thoughts interact with each other.

The scientific approach deals only with sensory experiences (past and present), and with logic and reason. Aristotle advocated this approach, which forms the basis of modern science's evidence-based, empirical reasoning. The intuitive approach consists of looking deep within the self. Plato advocated this method and used it to identify the cardinal virtues. The person becomes aware of the universal categories of truth, beauty, justice, love, and being itself. The "highest" of these has been called "the good" and "the oneness."

The approaches are based on different paradigms. The scientific approach relies on perception (experience), space, time, energy, matter, causation, measurement, replication, and the human mind using logic and reason. Intuition is used to recognize possibilities that may be tested by the scientific method. The intuitive method relies on these and the additional categories of *intention* and *non-material agency* (e.g.: God, angels, the devil, or voodoo forces). This difference is the basis of the conflict between *evolution* and *intelligent design* in many communities today.

In everyday life there is a rich interplay between these two types of thinking.

Mythos and *Logos* Ways of Knowing

In religious history these two ways of thinking are often called *mythos* and *Logos*.[2] Mythos describes the beliefs of a culture expressed symbolically. Logos describes the world rationally, in concepts tangible and concrete. These two ways of perceiving and expressing can be seen as complementary paths of knowing.

Mythos, myths, and mysticism draw heavily from the unconscious mind. Because of the *primary-process* thinking involved, myths are not necessarily reasonable or rational. Myths speak to and from our subconscious and unconscious minds.

The Logos is logical, rational, and forward-looking. Coming predominately from the conscious mind, it is the basis of all science. It includes factual history. However, Logos cannot assuage pain, sorrow, or guilt. It can explain the facts of a tragedy, but cannot use them to abate the resulting sense of grief.

Before the scientific era, which began about 1500 CE, mythos was more prominent. It dealt with myths about meaning, essentially meaning about existential issues. It gave explanations from the past, of how things came to be the way they are. The world was seen as "alive" with spirits. Every force such as storms, the sea, life, growth, agriculture, war, and romantic love had a god or goddess who was responsible for it. People hit by Cupid's arrows fell in love, even if the relationship appeared ridiculous, just as it does with some couples today. As cities developed, each community had a spiritual patron. The prerogatives of these gods and goddesses were limited only by higher divinities and by fate.

> *Pluto, god of the underworld, abducted Persephone, daughter of Demeter, goddess of agriculture. Demeter was so upset by the loss of her daughter that she neglected her responsibilities for the crops. The Earth became a wasteland. People lacked food, and the gods went without sacrifices. As a result, the gods and goddesses implored Zeus to do something. Zeus pressured Pluto to return Persephone, but because she had eaten six pomegranate seeds, she was required to spend six months a year in the underworld. It is her absence from the Earth that results in winter.*[3]

Thinking Described Psychologically

Today the disciplines of psychology and psychiatry find this distinction helpful, calling them *primary-process thinking* and *secondary-process thinking*. Primary-process thinking is epitomized by the dream. Secondary-process thinking is epitomized by finding the solution to a math problem. These two types are similar to the two philosophical approaches to knowledge of Plato and Aristotle, and in the religious arena to mythos and Logos. Most everyday thinking is an interplay of the two. These two types of thinking seem to have a basis in the physiology of the brain. (See Chapter 7)

Primary Processing

Primary processing is a method of thought, a way of thinking, of processing our perceptions and ideas. It is characterized by at least seven qualities:

1. A part may be taken to represent the whole. For example, a window may represent an entire house. Even though we might see the Ultimate only in part, we can believe that part represents the whole.

2. Similarities may be taken as identical. Without similarities, transparency and transcendence could not occur. They have to be comparable to something that can be recognized. Sympathetic magic, including the voodoo doll, is dependent on the similarity of characteristics.

3. The whole may stand for one of its parts. For example, the house may represent a door. One aspect of the Holy seen by the mystic may stand for the entirety of the Ultimate, just as the cross may represent all of Christianity.

4. Opposites may be taken as identical. Opposites "pivot" around the same point. For example, love and hate are complements of the same infatuation, and thus may be perceived as interchangeable. It also accounts for how a couple may quarrel and reconcile easily.

5. Everything occurs in the present tense; there is no past or future. It deals only with perceptions as they occur. This aspect of primary-process thinking can help give immediacy and vividness to a mystical experience, making it compelling and leaving no room for doubt.

6. There is an absence of negation: "no," "not," "never," and similar grammatical negatives are never part of the description. It is limited only to what *is* as if it always is. The Ultimate reveals a legitimacy for itself, for the mystic, for the world, for everything. Nothing is a contradiction.

7. Logical contradictions do not cancel each other out; rather, they exist side by side without dissonance.

Primary-process thinking is heard in children's play. In adults it is used in allusions, analogies, displacements, and symbolic representations. Hence it is found in poetry, metaphors, sacred scriptures, and artistic paintings. It is also found in myths, legends, fairy tales, and shamanic practices.[4]

Secondary Processing

The secondary process is rational and logical. Contradictions are not acceptable. There is negation, and there are past and future tenses. With its more logical form, it provides clarity. It is the way of science, which is always open to review and to data collected different ways. Old data are subject to reinterpretation, which may lead to a new theory with explanations that are more complete and comprehensive.

Often the experiences and revelations seen in the primary process of dreams and mystical experiences undergo secondary elaboration and interpretation. Secondary-process principles are used to recast the experience, thereby making it seem more logical and coherent. However, critical elements are often ignored, covered up, or modified, sometimes to the point of gross distortions.

Religious Thought

With the intuitive or spiritual approach, the experience of focusing on a religious concept or object merges with mystical experiences. It is in mystical states that the unity, the "oneness" of all things, is recognized as eternal and unconditional, the Infinite, the Ultimate. This unity may be identified as God. Accordingly, the knowledge of God is thought to be intuitive, easily recognized when earnestly sought, self-evident, and so compelling that there is no room for doubt. This knowledge is also held to precede all other knowledge. The individual is then confronted with his or her own finiteness. All finite things, such as books, humans, and nations are specially bound and transitory. All contain some distortion, some imperfection.[5] The universal categories contain within themselves the specific and the finite. A person participates in the Ultimate by his/her finiteness being transparent to the Infinite, or to the Universal.[6]

Myths

A myth tells a special kind of story. Religious myths usually deal with existential questions:

> *What is death? What happens after death? What is life? What is life about? Why are we here? Where were we before we were born? What is birth? How did the world begin? What is evil? Why do we have evil in the world? What is goodness? Why am I here? How should I live my life? What is of value? Why do people get sick or hurt? Why do people die? How do we deal with sorrow, grief, and guilt?*

There is a human neurological compulsion to come up with answers to these questions. Effective myths offer some resolution.

Myths decrease existential anxiety. They speak to our unconscious minds and involve primary-process operations. Myths deal with what is thought to be constant in our existence, dealing with what is permanent or what recurs cyclically in life. Mystical knowledge is intuitive. Myths do not convey factual history, or practical reality; rather, they convey timeless standards for attitudes and behaviors within a society. Myths tell stories of the struggle between order and chaos, between good and evil. Myths convey truths perceived by the people who tell them, truths about how things are and why they are that way. The language of myth, like the language of poetry, is metaphysical and symbolic. Symbolic language uses terms from everyday reality, but refers to the supernatural by analogy to everyday phenomena. All religions begin with myths. Not all religious myths are about gods and goddesses. Karen Armstrong reported that the Chinese worship ancestors and that the rituals honoring departed kin provide a model of the idealized social order. Myths are needed to help infuse the spirit of compassion and the sacredness of life. They are needed to help people venerate the world as sacred.[7] If a myth does not give its hearers a deeper insight into the meaning of life, it has failed, and it will not endure. However, if the myth forces people to change their hearts and minds, if it gives new hope and compels them to live more fully, it is a valid myth, and it will endure.[8] As a society changes, myths may become irrelevant, losing their power to speak to the hearts of its people. When a myth ceases to give people intimations of transcendence, it is forgotten and discarded, or it is considered abhorrent.[9] There is no orthodox version of a myth. Different myths are needed at different times and under different circumstances. The same is true for religious symbols.[10]

Historical Events and Stories Transformed to Myths

Myths are not about history or theology, but rather about human experience, gods, and the world bound together.[11] The following is from Karen Armstrong's *A Short History of Myth*.[12]

> Unless an historical event is mythologized, it cannot become a source of inspiration. A myth...is an event that in some sense happened once, but which also happens all the time. An occurrence needs to be liberated, as it were, from the confines of a specific period and brought into the lives of contemporary worshipers... The rituals of the Passover have for centuries made this tale central to the spiritual lives of Jews, who are told that each and every one of them must consider himself to be of the generation that escaped from Egypt. A myth cannot be correctly understood without a transforming ritual, which brings it into the lives and hearts of generations of worshipers. A myth demands action: the myth of the Exodus demands that Jews cultivate an appreciation of freedom as a sacred value, and refuse either to be enslaved themselves or to oppress others. By ritual practice and ethical response, the story has ceased to be an event in the distant past, and has become a living reality.

St. Paul did the same with Jesus... (In 2nd Corinthians 5:16 Paul wrote:) "Even if we did once know Christ in the flesh, that is not how we know him now." What was important was the "mystery" of his death and resurrection. Paul had transformed Jesus into the timeless, mystical hero who dies and is raised to a new life... Everybody that went through the initiation of baptism entered into Jesus's death and would share his new life. Jesus was no longer a mere historical figure but a spiritual reality in the lives of Christians by means of ritual and ethical discipline of living the same selfless life as Jesus himself. Christians no longer knew him "in the flesh" but they would encounter him in other human beings, in the study of scripture, and in the Eucharist. They knew that this myth was true, not only because of the historical evidence, but because they *had* experienced transformation. Thus the death and "rising up" of Jesus was a myth: it happened once to Jesus and was now happening all the time.[13]

Myths encourage going beyond everyday experiences. They must lead to imitation or participation, not to passive contemplation.[14] Most myths have unrealistic and/or unnatural happenings that call for suspending the sense of reality, just as fairy tales and fantasy fiction do. Myths are intended to provide an explanation for those divine moments that people sometimes experience. The story and the ritual together engender feelings of spirituality. They reduce the distance from the Divine, and they turn religious ideas into emotional experiences.[15]

Sacred Revelations and the Use of Symbols

The interpretation the Hebrews placed on historical events was sometimes taken as divine revelation. For others, sacred revelation often originates in a mystical experience. The result of either technique is seeing a part of the Ultimate and realizing there is more. Sometimes insight is passed to others in oral or written form. As soon as Mohammad returned from a mystical experience, he recounted it to his wife, who wrote it down. This collection of writings is now known as the *Qur'an.*

The transcendent aspects of revelatory descriptions are recognized and cherished by others who hear or read them. Without the transcendence aspect, however, these insights have little or no relevancy for the mystic or for others. The hearers may take the mystic's description or the symbols of the description and make them into mere objects of devotion rather than references to the

Divine. Unfortunately, those who receive this message often merge the specific with the transcendent aspects and hold on to the finite as strongly and devotedly as they hold and revere the transcendent.[16, 17]

On the other hand, myths can concentrate too much on the supernatural without enough emphasis on human aspects to be meaningful to their audience. Myths need to be primarily concerned with humanity.[18, 19] For myths to endure, they must be meaningful to the people.

Needing to Revere Something Greater

Generally, there would seem to be a need to give oneself to, or to worship something greater than, the self. In varying contexts, that something may be referred to as God, the Ultimate, the Unconditional, the Infinite, the Universal, or Nature. Worship can take many forms. Perhaps living a life that is transparent to the Infinite is the most authentic religious way to live. Such a life would be harmoniously transparent to the Infinite in feeling, in thought, and in action. The will to be open in this way is symbolically articulated in the Christian Lord's Prayer: "Thy will be done on earth as it is in heaven."[20] The concept is also intrinsic to Islam. The very word "Islam" means surrendering to the will of Allah.

The embodiment of an ultimate concern, of course, always occurs within finite realities. Religious symbols are always embedded in the finite. Therefore, religious symbols intrinsically lack absolute truth, but they are—or once were—transparent to the Infinite. The use of religious symbols is found in sacred scripture, myths, or key words; or in images, stories, legends, rituals, creeds, doctrines, rules, principles, or ideals for life. These symbols may well contribute to the teachings of a religion, and may help people understand what they experience, believe, or do. Myths go far to create the awareness that behind the appearance a mystery exists that involves both the timeless Ultimate and the finiteness of people.

Tillich pointed out that symbols may lose their transparency to the Infinite, especially as a society changes, and that people need to search continuously for new, clearer, and more meaningful symbols that reflect the Infinite. Otherwise, these symbols become mere signs or fossils, and they lose their power. He states that current symbols which are transparent to the Ultimate are absolutely necessary to preserve the vitality of a religion.[21]

NOTES FOR CHAPTER THREE

3.1   See Chapter Seven, "The Neocortex"

3.2   Armstrong, Karen: *The Battle for God*, Ballantine Publishing Group, New York, 2001

3.3   Seyffert, Oskar: *The Dictionary of Classical Mythology, Religion, Literature and Art*, Gramercy Books, distributed by Random House, 1995, P. 472

3.4   Hinsie, Leland E., M.D.; and Robert J. Campbell: *Psychiatric Dictionary*, 4th Ed, Oxford University Press, NYC, London and Toronto, 1970, p. 591

3.5   Brown, D. MacKenzie: *Ultimate Concern, Tillich in Dialogues*, Harper and Row, New York City, 1965, p. 49 & 55

3.6   Tillich, Paul: *A History of Christian Thought*, Touchstone Books, Simon & Schuster, NY, 1967 p. xxxii

3.7   See Chapter Twelve

3.8   Armstrong, Karen: *A Short History of Myth*, Conongate, New York City, 2005, p. 136-7

3.9   Armstrong: *A Short History of Myth*, p. 10

3.10   Armstrong: *A Short History of Myth*, p. 94

3.11   See Chapter Nine

3.12   Armstrong: *A Short History of Myth*, p. 5

3.13   Armstrong: *A Short History of Myth*, p. 106

3.14   *Bible*: 2 Corinthians 5:16

3.15   Armstrong: *A Short History of Myth*, p. 135

3.16   Newberg, Andrew, M.D.; d'Aquili, Eugene, M.D.; Rause, Vince: *Why God Won't Go Away*, Ballantine Books, New York City, 2001, p. 90 & 91

3.17   Schleiermacher, Friedrich: *Dr. Religion*, Tice, Terrence N., trans., Knox Press, Richmond, VA, 1969, p. 94

3.18   See Chapter Ten, "Confabulation"

3.19   Armstrong: *A Short History of Myth*, p. 19-21

3.20   *Bible*: Matthew 6:10

3.21   Tillich

CHAPTER FOUR

Religious Action

Like all organizations, religious organizations engage in two kinds of actions. The obvious kind are actions that further their missions, their "causes." The other kind is not always so obvious. These actions are for preserving and protecting the organization itself, actions meant to ensure that it survives for the long-term.

In individuals, good actions are considered *virtuous*. Avoiding bad actions is also considered virtuous. For example, Hindus hold that true religion is found in positive actions such as forgiveness, honesty, and justice; and in avoiding negative actions such as theft, abuse, and murder. Hindus believe that God commands mortal men to practice these virtues, which add up to *dharma*, another word for religion.[1]

Jesus stressed the importance of actions: "But if I do them, even though you do not believe me, believe the works so that you may know and understand that the Father is in me, and I am in the Father."[2]

Examples of religious actions include giving charity ("giving of alms"), reading sacred scripture, preaching and listening to sermons, praying, reciting liturgy, playing religious music, and singing religious songs. Some religions include dancing. Some include eating or abstaining from certain foods. Going to war or refusing to go to war are considered by many to be religious actions. Pilgrimages or missions, such as the Muslim Hajj, are deemed religious actions, as is the two years of missionary service required of Mormons by the Church of Jesus Christ of Latter-day Saints. Participating in rituals, making offerings or sacrifices, attending services, and practicing acts of private and communal service are expected of followers by their religious organizations.

Other actions are symbolic, such as bowing, kneeling, crossing, or touching the head in order to acknowledge superiority of the deity. Some require maintaining a certain symbolic appearance, such as clothing and hairstyles. Some have even required scarring the body, which is both painful and irreversible.

People often want to help others because they feel compassion, even love. This kind of action creates *secondary feelings*, such as closeness, openness, gratitude, generosity, devotion, faithful trust in one's values, and confidence. These secondary feelings include the reward of living up to one's ideals in feeling, thought, and action. This is the feeling of being in harmony.

Harmony is what this book is all about.

Rituals

From birth through death, everybody participates in rituals. Rituals may be secular or religious. Even secular rituals are often rooted in religious ones. For example, many of the practices in secular wedding ceremonies and funeral services include practices developed for religious reasons.

The ultimate object of religious rituals is securing a full life and escaping from evil.[3] Humans need to find meaning, and rituals serve to enhance the importance of key events. The meaninglessness that we perhaps fear most is death, but cultural beliefs and practices reassure us that we will find meaning beyond death. Rituals, along with symbols, are important ways for people to feel as if they are transcending death.[4]

Rituals are the performance of pre-set actions and/or sayings that do not even have to be entirely understood by the participants.[5] They are rites or ceremonies to sustain and enhance life. At the mundane level, they are called habits or customs, such as shaking hands or reciting a pledge. Rituals guide us in our behavior toward others and in their reactions to us. Although rituals vary by culture and over time, the very nature of our need for them is universal. It is also plausible that the most common messages in our rituals are also universal.[6]

Rituals give drama to concepts. They add emotional depth. They elevate even simple ideas to the level of great feeling. They help us share those feelings with each other. Sometimes we are aware of rituals' purposes, sometimes not. Consider three ways that rituals help us cope with the mystery of our existence.

1. **Establish Identity:** Rituals establish group identity and give each member a sense of belonging. They help the group achieve solidarity. They convey to current members information from the group's past. They express the meaning of belonging to a family, group, community, nation, or religion. Rituals help people understand where they fit within the larger scheme, and they help members relate to others who are in the group as well as those who are not. The mating ritual likely emerged as one of the earliest in our evolution. These are found even among insects, birds, and lower mammals. They identify the species and the gender.

2. **Contribute to Sense of Order:** Some rituals contribute to a sense of order, a way of reassuring during periods of change and upheaval. Rituals ground people in that which endures. They imply that all other conventions and interpretations are incorrect, or even unnatural.[7] Religious rituals aspire to help each person make contact with whatever is good, true, and beautiful. Rituals provide specific points of view from which each person can comfortably watch the world change. Beware, though, that rituals for this purpose can also express intolerance and hatred.

3. **Help Cope With Uncertainty:** When people experience big transitions—birth, religious growth, graduation, marriage, rewarded accomplishments, retirement, and the deaths of loved ones—rituals answer questions and give direction. Death is one of the greatest uncertainties we face. Rituals for dealing with death reassure us that we matter to loved ones, that life continues and is valued. Religious death rituals reassure many that life continues in other forms beyond death. Rituals establish common behaviors for people experiencing grief. All rituals are humanity's basic social actions.

Rituals Bridge the Divine and Human Worlds

Rituals connect the literal to the symbolic. They relate the finite to the Infinite or Universal. Linking death to a spiritual afterlife works this way. This is an example of primary-process identification.[8] While religious actions such as prayer generate feelings of closeness to others who are praying, the main goal is to connect with the Infinite.

Rituals and prayers take different forms, depending on their intent. They might be to praise, to offer thanks, to make requests for oneself or others, or to assist the deity in tasks, such as how the Mayans prayed to make sure the sun would rise tomorrow. The Australian aborigines have long believed that completing their rituals without interruption maintains the cosmic order.[9] In some societies, rituals have even intended to control or direct the deity, or to control the future.

Sacrifice Is a Measure of Value

Sacrifice often accompanies rituals. The sacrifice is a transfer of value. While it passes along the value of whatever is given, it also proves that the giver is committed to the purpose of the ritual.[10] If the value of the sacrifice is small, the commitment is considered shallow, or not worth very much. The greater the value of the sacrifice, the more the giver's intent is considered great.

After the death of King Ahab, the new king and the people of Moab revolted against Israel. A combined Israeli-Judean force moved to subdue Moab. The tide of war was going against Moab. Then the king of Moab took his eldest son, who would succeed him, and offered him as a whole sacrifice to their god, Chemosh, upon the city's wall in clear view of both armies. In those days it was thought that gods were territorial. The battle was on Moab's soil, not Israel's or Judea's. The sacrifice had a positive moral effect on the Moabite army. It so filled the Israeli-Judean army with consternation that they struck their camp and returned to their own lands.[11]

The educational and organizational activities of a religious community are rituals. This includes the participation of both the religious leaders and the members of the church. For example, rituals of purification often involve water: washing, bathing, immersion, or sprinkling. Blood may create the need for ritual purification, or may be cleansing in itself. The initiation for joining a congregation often includes a ritual symbolizing death and rebirth, such as baptism. Rituals may be conditional, restricted in time, or continual. Verbal rituals may be associated with eating, such as "saying grace." Clothing may have religious significance. Primitive peoples have used tattoos and skin scarification. Male circumcision as a religious ritual is practiced by Jews, Muslims, and others. Some societies have even used human sacrifice as religious ritual.

New Rituals Often Incorporate Older Ones

When new rituals come about, they tend to be composed of elements from earlier rituals or rituals imported from other societies.[12] Will Durant noted that often rituals are more difficult to change than beliefs.[13]

The pious Arabs of Arabia had trekked to the Kaaba in Mecca long before Mohammed. He continued the custom because he did not want to alienate the merchants of Mecca, and because he knew that rituals are not as easy to change as beliefs.[14] By accepting the older rite, he reduced people's resistance to accepting Islam throughout Arabia. Christianity also includes a history of incorporating the rituals of others. For example, Christ Mass was designated to celebrate the birth of Jesus in order to bring new meaning to the pagan Yule celebration of the winter-solstice rebirth of the sun.

Sometimes a ritual seems to begin without the feeling component, yet it is expected to help generate the desired feelings. Dancing in unison as a group usually generates feelings of uniting everybody's mind, heart, body, and community.

Accord, harmony, and unification are strengthened.[15] In tribal societies, the whole village participates in rituals, which helps strengthen the group identify. After a time, this blurs the distinction between individuals and the group.[16]

Participation

Participation is the key to successful rituals. Refusing to participate in an important ritual sets oneself apart from the group. Participation in a public ritual proves one's public commitment to accepting the ritual's meaning. Unlike passively hearing the stories or watching a dramatization, participating is an action that confirms one's feelings. Because Socrates refused to participate in certain rituals, he was accused of treason for not worshiping the gods of the city, which set a bad example and corrupted the youth. Ritual does not prove belief, but rather confirms accepting the message. Ritual participation often symbolizes an agreement, the breaking of which may be considered an immoral act.[17]

Reliable Means of Creating Numinous Experiences

Rappaport said ritual is the most reliable means of having numinous experiences—feelings of the Divine—as described by Rudolf Otto.[18] It generates feelings of oneness with others, with one's partner, the congregation, the village or nation, and with God. "The goal of the contemplative rituals practiced by some Catholic mystics, for example, is to attain the state of the *Unio Mystica*, the mysterious union that the mystic experiences as a sense of union with the actual presence of God. In Buddhism, the aim of meditative rituals is to encounter the ultimate oneness of everything by defeating the limiting sense of self generated by the ego."[19] The aim of religious rituals is to transcend the self and identify with something greater, such as the group or God. This is the mysterious union.[20]

Rituals aid in turning ideas into divine emotional experiences.[21] This contributes to the feeling among participants of certainty, of proof the experience is divine.[22] Virtually every cult and every religion has rituals.[23]

To maintain the feelings rituals create among participants and the community as a whole, they need to be repeated fairly often. Islam prescribes five rituals per day in the form of prostration, prayer, and the saying, "There is no God but Allah and Mohammed is his messenger." These brief rituals bring divine presence to everyday experience. Lengthy rituals lift people out, and attempt to impose order in, the physical world.[24]

The Non-variable Effect of Meaningful Popular Rituals

When a ritual that attempts to control or make requests of the supernatural fails to achieve the desired result, it is assumed to have been performed improperly. Rituals often contain Ultimate Sacred Postulates, such as "There is no God but Allah and Mohammed is his messenger," or the Jewish Schema, in abbreviated form: "Hear O Israel, the Lord our God, the Lord is one."[25] Ultimate Sacred Postulates cannot be falsified, nor can they be verified. They are considered unquestionable.[26] The lack of variance in repeated rituals, combined with their perception as representing Ultimate Sacred Postulates, gives them sanctity. Congregations do not question rituals with sanctity. Rituals and myths need to occur together for their greatest meaning and impact. Rituals provide certainty and order in the world. They reassure that not all is chaos.[27] A ritual's meaningfulness depends more on the receiver's openness than on its message.[28] Rhythm and body movement increase receptivity. Meaningfulness is enhanced when one's heart (feelings), mind (thought), and body (action) are all in harmony.[29]

Rituals may be used for evil. In general, the intent of evil rituals falls into four categories:

1. To harm others, such as in voodoo or "casting a spell" to cause injury or misfortune;

2. To dominate or control others, such as holding public executions or cutting the hair of captured natives;

3. To raise an object not considered divine, such as *idolatry*;

4. To fragment or violate something sacred, such as church-bombing or acts of terrorism.[30]

Sanctity always supports social order.[31] The truth of sanctity is generally stronger than the truth of experience.[32]

Language

Talking is considered action. The development of language gave humans considerable survival advantage over species without language. Language allows the growth of abstract concepts such as good and evil. Other examples include imaginary beings—demons, dinji, leprechauns, guardian angels, gods, and other spirits—and abstract places or states of being such as heaven, hell, and life after death. Being able to manipulate abstract concepts makes it easier to dominate the people who believe them. For example, people who fear voodoo spells can be controlled by voodoo threats, while those who do not believe in voodoo would ignore such threats.

Language Creates Two Potential Problems for Religious Authorities

While language offers benefits to people and societies, it also allows people to grasp two potentially problematic concepts: outright lies, and alternatives to accepted ideas.[33] While rituals tend to unite people, language can be used to divide them.[34] Being able to think and speak of alternative ideas may be the first step toward challenging authority and even disrupting the order of society.[35] Societies tend to recognize this threat and thus try to protect themselves. Consider the Protestant Reformation, which began with writing and posting 95 themes. Heretics—those who have rejected accepted teachings—have long been regarded as even more evil than infidels, who have not yet learned and accepted common religious beliefs. This is why the Inquisition arose to respond to heresy. Freedom *from* religion can be more important than freedom *of* religion.

The Axial Age, New Prescriptions for Action

Perhaps the greatest historical change in religious action occurred in what Karl Jaspers referred to as "the Axial Age" in his book, *The Way of Wisdom*.[36] From 800 BCE to 200 BCE, but mainly in the 6th century BCE, these changes occurred throughout the civilized world, from China, India, and Persia (Iran) to Judea (Israel) and later to Greece.[37] Before then, most religions focused on the role of people using rituals, prayers, and sacrifice to help gods maintain order in the universe. Examples include the seasons' effects on crops, and the cycles of the sun, moon, and zodiac.[38] The Axial Age brought new emphasis on how people related to each other, such as compassion, honesty, forgiveness, and social justice—in other words, morals and ethics. With this shift, tribe or clan identity also shifted more toward individual identity.

Zarathustra of Persia (now Iran), founder of Zoroastrianism, believed that life was a struggle between the forces of good and evil. The god Ahura Mazda was deemed wholly good, while the god Ahriman was totally evil. Prior to Zarathustra, few societies believed in individual existence after death. Those few that did tended not to link afterlife with actions made during life. Rather, the afterlife depended on whether or not the person or his whole community pleased the gods with sufficient rituals and sacrifices. Heroic deeds were considered a factor.[39]

In Hinduism, the Vedas predated the Axial Age. They mainly dealt with rituals, prayers, hymns, and sacrifices.[40] The Bhagavad-Gita, another sacred text of

Hinduism written later in the Axial Age, addressed existential questions about the meaning of life and death. The Vedas and Bhagavad-Gita described a common theme: the world was created by the gods sacrificing themselves.[41]

Taoism, Confucianism, Buddhism, and Jainism were developed in the Axial Age. In Jewish history, it was the time of Jeremiah and other prophets around the time of the Babylonian captivity. The Axial Age came to Greece somewhat later with the rise of the philosophy of Socrates, Plato, and Aristotle.

In *The Great Transformation* Karen Armstrong wrote that religion in the Axial Age showed little interest in doctrines or metaphysics. [42] Religion was about action that changed people at a profound level. Morality was the core of spiritual life. King Asoka, third ruler of India's Mauryan dynasty (c. 300 B.C. to c. 232 B.C.) is a good example. Perhaps the second-most influential Buddhist in history, he defeated the east-coast state of Kalinga (presently Orissa), but withdrew in remorse over the shocking human price of the war: 100,000 killed, plus more wounded. He renounced all war and adopted Buddhism to practice the virtues of *dharma*, including truthfulness, mercy, and non-violence. Although be promoted Buddhism, he ensured that all religions would be tolerated. During his 68-year reign, Buddhism grew from a local philosophy mainly in northwest India to a popular nationwide religion spreading to other countries.[43]

Religious scholars debate weather Taoism and Confucianism should be considered religions or just systems of ethics. Buddhism is widely considered a religion. None of the three believe in gods. All three have sacred texts. All three provide a philosophy of life, an explanation for our place in the world. Their texts and ethics are their objects of devotion.

Axial Age sages did not impose their views of ultimate reality on others, and even discouraged accepting religious teachings on faith alone. They encouraged people to question everything and test religion against their own personal experiences. First, one must commit to an ethical life. Then the actions of regular benevolence, not just belief in it, would lead to transcendence. They preached a spirituality of empathy and compassion. They advocated expanding benevolence beyond one's own people in order to extend it to the entire world. Most of the great religious traditions emerged around this time, including the supreme importance of charity to others. It is very meaningful to realize that our values about living life are so deeply in accord with others.

Social Justice

Social-justice issues guiding actions were a major cause for the changes of the Axial Age. The biblical scriptures themselves give reasons for the change. This is most strikingly stated by Israel's prophets, notably Isaiah, Jeremiah, Amos, Hosea, and Micah. In their roles as spokesmen of the Lord God, they reflected transformation of their god from a tribal god, who could be influenced by burnt offerings to intervene supernaturally in human affairs, into a god of a whole people, even of the whole world, who wrote the message of compassion and social justice on the hearts of Israel. The following plea from the Psalms reflects this shift:

> How long will you judge unjustly and show partiality to the wicked? Give justice to the weak and the orphan; maintain the right of the lowly and the destitute. Rescue the weak and the needy: deliver them from the hand of the wicked.[44]

The following two statements by Isaiah and Jeremiah dramatize the great shift, in situations where both leaders and people are breaking their historic covenant with God:

> Hear the word of the Lord, you rulers of Sodom! Listen to the teaching of our God, you people of Gomorrah! What to me is the multitude of your sacrifices? says the Lord; I have had enough of burnt offerings of rams and the fat of fed beasts; I do not delight in the blood of bulls, or of lambs, or of goats. When you come to appear before me, who asked this from your hand? Trample my courts no more; bringing offerings is futile; incense is an abomination to me. New moon and sabbath and calling of convocation—I cannot endure solemn assemblies with iniquity. Your new moons and your appointed festivals my soul hates; they have become a burden to me, I am weary of bearing them. When you stretch out your hands, I will hide my eyes from you; even though you make many prayers, I will not listen; your hands are full of blood. Wash yourselves; make yourselves clean; remove the evil of your doings from before my eyes; cease to do evil, learn to do good; seek justice, rescue the oppressed, defend the orphan, plead for the widow.[45]

> Woe to him who builds his house by unrighteousness, and his upper rooms by injustice; who makes his neighbors work for nothing, and does not give them their wages; who says, "I will build myself a spacious house with large upper rooms," and who cuts out windows for it, paneling it with cedar, and painting it with vermilion. Are you

a king because you compete in cedar? Did not your father eat and drink and do justice and righteousness? Then it was well with him. He judged the cause of the poor and needy; then it was well. Is not this to know me? says the Lord. But your eyes and heart are only on your dishonest gain, for shedding innocent blood, and for practicing oppression and violence.[46]

Justice is at the core of the Judeo-Christian view of the world and of God. This view of justice has had a major impact on Christianity and Islam, as well as Judaism. Ethics has been an integral part of most religions ever since. Since the impetus for religious ethics is essentially the same among the religions, their ethics are similar. The greatest difference is how big are their circles of inclusion.

Ethical Systems

Religions develop systems of ethics to guide actions. In addition to ethics toward fellow humans, religions commonly add guidance for how to relate to the Divine. The Ten Commandments is the system developed by the Hebrews.[47] The first four commandments deal with relating to God. Number five specifies one's proper attitude toward parents. The other five deal with relating to other people, including those who may be older or younger, or a friend, stranger, or foe. The relationship is critical because it determines whether the other person is—or should be—within one's circle of concern. These commandments, plus obedience to the word of God, are sanctioned at times by negative consequences for the individual or for the community. When a community believes it is likely to be punished by a higher power, peer pressure to conform increases.

> *Before the battle for Jericho, God had commanded that the troops take no plunder. All plunder was to be deposited in the store house of the Lord. One man broke that order. As a result the entire Hebrew army was routed. That man was identified and was stoned to death. When the battle was resumed, the Hebrews won.*[48]

The Axial Age saw the rise of quite a few ethical systems. In Judaism, eternal life depends on one's relationship with God. Israel's entire history has depended on Hebrews honoring their commitment to God to live a moral and ethical life. Each generation of every nation has to decide for or against righteousness. Deciding against righteousness results in self-destruction. [49]

Afterlife Beliefs Reinforce Ethics

Because people dislike seeing others get away with evil acts, the concept of sanctions after death grew and became increasingly elaborate. To be effective in guiding actions, the individual must believe in the system, and the "judge" has to know the person's history of good and bad deeds. This means the judge must be omniscient, so nobody can conceal sins. The anticipated rewards and punishments must be known during life. Similar ideas are found in many cultures. For example, Santa Claus is portrayed as an omniscient judge weighing children's deeds as "naughty" or "nice."

Two systems for this became popular over the past few millennia. One is based on the concepts of karma and reincarnation, as found in Hinduism, Buddhism, and Jainism. The other, which is the basis of Christianity, sends people to heaven or hell for good deeds or bad. Hinduism arose early in the Axial Age with the Upanishads. With *reincarnation*, a person's earthly existence is but one in a series of lifetimes. *Karma* is the weighing of good deeds minus bad deeds to determine one's position in the next life, which might be an insect, an animal, or a human. In India, the caste system is believed by Hindus to result from karma, determining one's rebirth into the four castes ranging from Brahman, the highest, to "untouchable," the lowest. The amount of karma one has will be increased or decreased by the choices made during life. Were they ethical and moral? Were they kind, considerate, and compassionate—or detrimental to others?

Buddhism grew out of Hinduism, much as Christianity grew out of Judaism. However, Buddhists do not have castes. While they do believe in reincarnation, their concept of karma is that when enough good is amassed, a person may be released from the otherwise endless cycle of rebirth. That release is the achievement of *nirvana*, the end of suffering, the full attainment of a blissful state.

Both Christianity and Islam believe in an afterlife in heaven (paradise) or hell. Reaching heaven requires believing and faith, as well as making ethical choices. Catholicism adds a possible interim state called purgatory, a temporary condition allowing purification so one can enter heaven. In all forms of Christianity, the possibility of going to hell acts as the deterrent. Belief in after-death consequences strengthens religions' call for moral behavior. It completes the system by making justice the final standard of a person and his incarnations for all eternity.

Global Ethics

In the 19th and 20th centuries we have come to recognize a global ethic. In 1785, Immanuel Kant wrote *Metaphysics of Morals*, in which he introduced his *categorical imperative*: "Act only on that maxim through which you can at the same time will that it becomes a universal law." Later he added: "Act so that you always use humanity, in your own person, as well as in the person of every other, never merely as a means, but at the same time as an end." Kant's rules had some exceptions, such as killing in self-defense. John Rawls pointed out that those exceptions occur when the rights of one person limits the rights of others. He proposed this principle: "Everyone is to be accorded the maximum liberty consistent with the liberty of others." Tillich cited Kant's statement that religion is only a tool for the fulfillment of the moral imperative.[50]

The Council of the Parliament of the World's Religions addressed the idea of universal ethics at a meeting in Chicago, summer 1993. 6,500 people from every religion worked out a "Declaration Toward a Global Ethic." They started by saying that this document and any they offer in the future are not intended to replace the high ethical standards of individual religions. They concluded:

- The global ethic must be grounded in the religions, for right without morality cannot long endure. Religion is needed because a global order cannot be created or maintained by laws, prescriptions, and conventions alone.
- Every human being should be treated humanely.
- Everyone should practice the Golden Rule.

They also committed themselves to a culture of:

- Non-violence and respect for human life.
- Solidarity and just economic order.
- Tolerance and truthfulness.
- Equal rights and partnership between men and women, and where sexuality should be creative and life affirming. It can only be effective when partners accept the responsibility of caring for each other's happiness.[51]

They also asserted that:

- There can be no peace in the world without peace among the religions.
- There can be no peace without agreement to solve social conflicts without violence.
- There can be no peace in the world without global justice.

- There can be no global justice in the world without truthfulness and humaneness.
- There is no need for a single religion, but global norms of ethical values are needed.
- Only the unconditional (God) can impose an unconditional obligation.[52]

Compassion

This concern for others gave rise to recognizing the value of compassion, as well as ethics. The Buddha had grown up as a prince in a luxurious palace. His father shielded him from knowledge of all suffering: disease, hunger, deprivation, and even death. As he gradually became aware of suffering compared to the life he had lived, he developed a deep compassion for others. Founding the religion of Buddhism, he became known as the Compassionate One.

Awareness of suffering and the response of compassion arose in much of the civilized world. Leaders sensitive to suffering questioned its causes. Religious institutions increasingly expressed concern for how adherents treated one another. Religious leaders were advocating actions to improve conditions for everyone. Four types of rules emerged:

1. Some form of the Golden Rule, "Do unto others as you would have them do to you" and its corollary, "Love your neighbor as yourself." (*Bible*: Galatians 5:14 NIT)

2. Related acts of goodwill such as the giving of alms (charity). The giving of alms can go awry in two extremes. One is giving alms for "show" and self-aggrandizement, recognition and respect from others. The other is to give alms with pity. Pity is an attitude of superiority toward the one who is deemed inferior, which is condescending, and denies love. Giving alms lovingly requires sympathy or empathy: "There but for the grace of God go I."

3. Striving for more forms of social justice.

4. Forgiveness of others' sins, transgressions against us.

People find spirituality and increased self-esteem in acts of compassion and in being helpful, honest, and fair; or in any of the four kinds of actions mentioned above. This form of spirituality is also found in the kind helpfulness of many aboriginal peoples in dealing with strangers from the outside world. It, too, appears to be universal.

Further, these prescriptions for living are ancient. Hindus define the God-spirit as being universal, eternal, and the creator of the universe. God is without form and name, but so God can be understood by common people he is given human form and attributes.

Arya-Dharma of Zoroastrianism represents the highest ideals in human-kind, namely to propagate the message of love and brotherhood among all men. True religion is found among those who practice forgiveness (except for the enemies of religion); those who refrain from theft, anger, murder; and those who are honest, disciplined, charitable, and just toward other humans.[53]

Both the Hindus and the Greek Stoics held that there is a divine spark within each human. This is the basis for the Hindus bowing to everyone they meet. The Greeks called this divine spark "reason." They believed other concepts were also inherent in all humans. They called these universal, built-in concepts "natural law." Natural law included the ability to recognize cosmic truth, goodness, and evil (e.g.: murder is wrong), and the Golden Rule.[54] Truth and goodness are two of Plato's transcendent values. The others are beauty and justice.

All religions encourage people to discover our universal capacity for *feeling* compassion. Recognizing the needs of others becomes *thought*. As we are moved to bring others into our circles of concern, only then are we inevitably moved to *action*.

NOTES FOR CHAPTER FOUR

4.1   Monroe, Charles: *World Religions, An Introduction*, Prometheus Books, Amherst, New York, 1995, p. 83

4.2   *Bible*: John 10:38

4.3   Becker, Ernest: *Escape From Evil*, Hocart, A.M., cited by, The Free Press Division of Simon & Schuster, New York City, 1975

4.4   Rappaport, Roy A.: *Rituals and Religion in the Making of Humanity*, Cambridge University Press, United Kingdom, 1999, p. 147

4.5   Rappaport: p. 24

4.6   Rappaport: p. 31

4.7   Rappaport: p. 438

4.8   See Chapter Three, "Thinking Described Psychologically"

4.9   Rappaport: p. 287

4.10   Rappaport: p. 142-4

4.11   *Bible*: 2 Kings 3:5-27

4.12   Rappaport: p. 32 & 436

4.13   Durant, Will: *The Story of Civilization, Vol 4, The Age of Faith*, Simon and Schuster, New York, 1950, p. 215

4.14   Durant: Vol 4, p. 215

4.15   Rappaport: p. 220

4.16   Rappaport: p. 380

4.17   Rappaport: p. 132

4.18   Rappaport: p. 70-74

4.19   Newberg, Andrew, M.D.; d'Aquili, Eugene, M.D.; Rause, Vince: *Why God Won't Go Away*, Ballantine Books, New York City, 2001, p. 80

4.20   Rappaport: p. 380

4.21   Newberg: p. 96

4.22 Newberg: p. 92

4.23 Rappaport: p. 209

4.24 Rappaport: p. 284

4.25 Rappaport: p. 277

4.26 Rappaport: p. 283

4.27 Rappaport: p. 286

4.28 Rappaport: p. 285

4.29 Rappaport: p. 220

4.30 Rappaport: p. 448

4.31 Rappaport: p. 427

4.32 Rappaport: p. 311

4.33 Rappaport: p. 321 & 415

4.34 Rappaport: p. 284

4.35 Rappaport: p. 322

4.36 Jaspers, Karl: *The Way of Wisdom*, Yale University Press, New Haven, CT, 1951

4.37 Muesse, Mark: *Religions of the Axial Age: An Approach to the World's Religions*, Lecture 1, The Teaching Co, Chantilly, VA,   2007

4.38 Muesse, Mark: *Religions of the Axial Age: An Approach to the World's Religions*, The Teaching Co, Chantilly, VA, 2007, p. 84

4.39 Muesse: p. 53

4.40 Muesse: p. 73

4.41 Muesse: p. 82

4.42 Armstrong, Karen: *The Great Transformation*; Alfred Knopf, New York, 2006, p. xiii-xv

4.43 Hart, Michael: *The 100: A Ranking of the Most Influential Persons in History*, Citadel Press by Carol Pub Group, 1996, p. 266

4.44 *Bible*: Psalms 82:2-4 New RSV

4.45 *Bible*: Isaiah 1:10-17

4.46 *Bible*: Jeremiah 22:13-17

4.47 *Bible*: Exodus 20

4.48 *Bible*: Joshua 6:18-25 and 7:21-26

4.49 Tillich, Paul: *Biblical Religion and The Search For Ultimate Reality*, University of Chicago Press, 1955, p. 44-46

4.50 Tillich, Paul: *A History of Christian Thought*, Touchstone Books, Simon & Schuster, New York, 1967, p. 388

4.51 Küng, Hans: *Global Responsibility, In Search of a New Ethic*, Crossroads Publishing Co., NYC, 1991, p. 18-32

4.52 Küng: p. xvi

4.53 Monroe, Charles: *World Religions, an Introduction*, Prometheus Books, Amherst, New York, 1995, p. 83

4.54 Wattles, Jeffery: *The Golden Rule*, Oxford University Press, 1996, p. 39 & 68

CHAPTER FIVE

Action in Scripture

The world's major religions are remarkably similar in the action they advocate. These similarities speak to our shared aspirations for the ideal of true social justice. Consider quotes from sacred scriptures of various religions regarding The Golden Rule, giving alms, social justice, and forgiveness of others.

The Golden Rule

Bhagavan Das, in *The Essential Unity of All Religions*, stated that The Golden Rule is found in all religions, worded positively or negatively.[1] He includes carillons of The Golden Rule of various religions. These include: "Hate never extinguishes hate. Only love can change hate to love," "Return good for evil," and "He who feels the joys and sorrows of others as his own is the true yogi. He has truly joined his soul with all souls."[2]

Hinduism: "Do not do to others what ye do not wish done to yourself; and wish for others too what ye desire and long for, for yourself—this is the whole of Dharma, heed it well." *Maha-bharata*. Some Hindus interpret The Golden Rule as an invitation to identify with the divine spirit within each person.[3]

Confucianism: Confucius was asked, "Is there a single word which can be a guide to conduct throughout one's life?" Confucius replied, "It is perhaps 'shu' (reciprocity). Do not impose on others what you do not desire."[4]

Buddhism: "Hurt not others in ways that you yourself would find hurtful."[5]

Jainism: "Treat all beings as he himself would be treated."[6]

Zoroastrianism: "That nature is only good which shall not do unto another, whatever is not good for its own self."[7]

Judaism: "Love your neighbor as yourself."[8] Jeffery Wattles repeats the story of a pagan who told Rabbi Hillel, "I will convert to Judaism if you will teach me the whole Torah while I stand on one foot." Hillel replied, "What is hateful to you, do not do unto others; that is the whole of the Torah, the rest is commentary; go and learn it."[9]

Christianity: "In everything do to others as you would have them do to you; for this is the law and the prophets."[10] The entire law is summed up in a single command: "Love your neighbor as yourself."[11] Paul referenced the concept of the natural law in regard to The Golden Rule in the *Bible*.[12] "Those who say, 'I love God,' and hate their brothers or sisters, are liars."[13]

Islam: "None of you believes (completely) until he loves for his brother what he loves for himself."[14] "Thou should like for others what thou likest for thyself; and what thou feelest painful for thyself hold that as painful for all others too."[15] al-Arabis gives instructions to a Postulant: "All commandments are summed up in this, that whatever you will like the True One to do to you, that do to His creatures, step by step."[16]

The Inca Indians of Peru: "Each one should do unto others as he would have others do unto him."[17]

Ba-Congo, Africa: "O man, what you not like, do not do to your fellows."[18]

Giving Alms (Charity)

Hinduism: The laws of Manu instruct the people in the rules of daily life. A Manu is expected to earn enough money to contribute to the state and the temple.[19] In the fourth stage of life, after retirement, the Hindu is expected to perform acts of charity and to help others less fortunate.[20] Moksha is the final path to union with Brahman. It is attained by a series of yoga. The second yoga, The Karma yoga, the path of action requires one to work faithfully, to practice charity, to do good deeds to others, to go on pilgrimages to holy places, and to live a selfless life.[21]

Jainism: "One must practice charity, give freely of one's wealth to aid the poor, build hospitals, homes for orphans, schools and temples."[22]

Judaism: The Jews were obligated to give a tenth, a tithe, of the products of their fields and of their herds each year. "All tithes from the land, whether the seed from the ground or the fruit from the tree, are the Lord's; they are holy to the Lord. All tithes of herd and flock, every tenth one that passes under the shepherd's staff, shall be holy to the Lord."[23] "Bring the full tithe into the store-house, so that there may be food in my house, and thus put me to the test, says the Lord of hosts; see if I will not open the windows of heaven for you and pour down for you an overflowing blessing."[24] Charity brings atonement.[25] The

Jews were the first people in the ancient world to establish a welfare system. It was the admiration of others.[26]

Christianity: "Whoever sows sparingly will also reap sparingly, and whoever sows generously will also reap generously. Each man should give what he has decided in his heart to give, not reluctantly or under compulsion, for God loves a cheerful giver. And God is able to make all grace abound to you, so that in all things at all times, having all that you need, you will abound in every good work. As it is written: 'He scatters abroad, he gives to the poor; his righteousness endures forever.'"[27] "So whenever you give alms, do not sound a trumpet before you, as the hypocrites do in the synagogues and in the streets, so that they may be praised by others. Truly I tell you they have received their reward. But when you give alms, do not let your left hand know what your right hand is doing, so that your alms may be done in secret; and your Father who sees in secret will reward you."[28] Also, the giving of alms is given as a justification for calling a man devout. "In Caesarea there was a man named Cornelius, a centurion of the Italian Cohort, as it was called. He was a devout man who feared God with all his household; he gave alms generously to the people and prayed constantly to God."[29] In Protestantism the sacrificial giving of alms is a means of grace, a way of experiencing God's love.

Islam: Giving of alms is one of the five pillars of Islam. Each year, the expected gift is two and a half percent of net worth. It is also a means of pleasing Allah.

Social Justice

Justice is one of the transcendent values that Plato stated could be discerned by an individual looking deep within the self. The famous laws of Hammurabi of Babylon, about the 18th century BCE, gave royal, feudal, legal, and social prescriptions, but were said to have been received from the god of justice.[30] Karen Armstrong, in *The History of God*,[31] said that the story of the Exodus of the Hebrews from Egypt, particularly as recorded in Deuteronomy 26, portrays God, Yahweh, on the side of the impotent and the oppressed:

> "The Egyptians ill-treated us. They gave us no peace, and inflicted harsh slavery upon us. But we called on Yahweh, the God of our fathers. Yahweh heard our voice and saw our misery, our toil, and oppression; and Yahweh brought us out of Egypt with a mighty hand and an outstretched arm, with great terror, and with signs and

wonders." Armstrong continued, "The God who may have inspired the first successful peasants' revolt in history is a God of revelation. In all three faiths (Judaism, Christianity, and Islam) he has inspired an ideal of social justice."

Buddhism: Buddha presented four Noble Truths; the fourth is the path to Nirvana, called the eightfold path. The path is more easily comprehended when reduced from 8 to 3: moral conduct, mental concentration, and wisdom. Further, murder and stealing, which includes bribery and cheating, are prohibited. One is to do an honest day's work—no loafing—and refrain from prostitution, alcohol, drugs, armaments, and slavery.[32]

Judaism: "Therefore because you trample on the poor and take from them levies of grain, you have built houses of hewn stone, but you shall not live in them; you have planted pleasant vineyards, but you shall not drink their wine. For I know how many are your transgressions, and how great are your sins—you who afflict the righteous, who take a bribe, and push aside the needy in the gate. Therefore the prudent will keep silent in such a time; for it is an evil time. Seek good and not evil, that you may live; and so the Lord, the God of hosts, will be with you, just as you have said."[33] Amos said that God would cut off ties with the nation, if it did not uphold justice.[34] "Woe to him who builds his house by unrighteousness, and his upper rooms by injustice; who makes his neighbors work for nothing, and does not give them their wages; who says 'I will build myself a spacious house with large upper rooms,' and who cuts out windows for it, paneling it with cedar, and painting it with vermilion. Are you a king because you compete in cedar? Did not your father eat and drink and do justice and righteousness? Then it was well with him. He judged the cause of the poor and needy, then it was well. Is not this to know me? says the Lord. But your eyes and heart are only on your dishonest gain, for shedding innocent blood, and for practicing oppression and violence."[35] "Those who oppress the poor insult their Maker, but those who are kind to the needy honor him."[36]

Islam: The life and property of all citizens in an Islamic state are considered sacred, whether a person is Muslim or not. Islam also protects honor. Racism is not allowed in Islam. Islam rejects the concept of certain individuals or nations being favored by God because of their wealth, power, or race. God created human beings as equals who are distinguished from each other only on the basis of their faith and piety. "Truly God commands you to give back trust to those to whom they are due, and when you judge between people, to judge with justice…"[37] "And act justly. Truly, Allah loves those who are just."[38] "And let not the hatred of others make you avoid justice. Be just: that is nearer to piety: and fear Allah…"[39]

Justice is a prerequisite for peace. There cannot be a permanently subjected people. That is unjust. Agitation will fester into covert violence, which will give way to open revolt. The 14th Amendment to the U.S. Constitution, passed shortly after the Civil War and the end of slavery, provides a framework within which equal rights for everyone under U.S. jurisdiction can be realized through organized, collective struggle.

Restorative Social Justice

There are at least two forms of social justice. One is *punitive* or *retributive justice*. The other is *restorative justice* in which the concern is the restoration of broken relationships, seeking to rehabilitate both the victim and the perpetrator, and to reintegrate them in the community. It is the work of healing, forgiveness, and reconciliation. This was the policy of the Truth and Reconciliation Commission chaired by Archbishop Desmond Tutu of South Africa.[40] Whether restorative justice begins with forgiveness or leads to it, religions recognize its importance in healing the wounds that inevitably arise among members of a community.

Forgiving Others

Taoism: Lao-tse: "Recompense injury with kindness."[41]

Sikhism: "Where there is forgiveness, there is God himself."[42]

Buddhism: "Never is hate diminished by hatred. It is only diminished by love. That is the eternal law."[43]

Judaism: "You shall not hate in your heart anyone of your kin; you shall reprove your neighbor, or you will incur guilt yourself. You shall not take vengeance or bear a grudge against any of your people, but you shall love your neighbor as yourself: I am the Lord."[44]

"By the time the Talmud was written, the idea of obedience to God, the king, had been extended to a powerful metaphor of decent relationships that humans owe each other. If all of us are subjects of the one transcendent King, then each of us owes the other the respect due an equal—and the redress due any equal we have damaged."[45] "Remorse toward God can bring forgiveness only for those hurts we have done toward God alone. We must try to make redress for those harms we have done to another human. And we must seek forgiveness from those people we have hurt. For many congregations, the first night of *slichot* has become a time for members of the community to come together to face the harms they have done each other, to apologize, to make redress and to seek each other's forgiveness. The root of forgiveness and reconciliation is the Root of Being."[46] Yom Kippur, the Day of Atonement, "effects atonement for transgressions between a person and God, but only if he has made peace with his fellows."[47]

There is a tradition that the evening service of Yom Kippur never ends. In some *Chavurah* congregations, this continuity has been expressed by ending the evening service with an open-ended meditation, the prayer of Chassidic Rebbe Levi Yitzzhak of Berditschev. They say individually:

> Lord of the World, I stand before You and before my neighbors pardoning, forgiving, struggling to be open to all who have hurt and angered me. Be this hurt of body or soul, of honor or property, whether they were forced to hurt me or did so willingly, whether by accident or intent, whether by word or deed, I forgive them because we are human. Let no one feel guilty on my account. I am ready to take upon myself the commandment, 'Love your neighbor as yourself.'

Each person remains in the prayer room, meditating until each feels satisfied, having fully forgiven those who have harmed him/her. They leave the room one by one as each reaches this point. Since the congregation as a whole never formally closes the service, the atmosphere of prayer and reconciliation continues, hovering in mid-air even after the last member leaves.[48]

Jainism: "Conquer your wrath with sweet forgiveness."[49]

Christianity: "But I say to you, Love your enemies and pray for those who persecute you."[50] "And forgive us our debts, as we also have forgiven our debtors."[51] "And forgive us our sins, for we ourselves forgive everyone indebted to us. And do not bring us to the time of trial."[52] "Bear with one another and, if anyone has a complaint against another, forgive each other; just as the Lord has forgiven you, so you also must forgive. Above all, clothe yourselves with love, which binds everything together in perfect harmony."[53]

Islam: "And vie with one another, hastening to forgiveness from your Lord, and a garden whose breadth is as the heavens and earth, prepared for the God fearing who expand in prosperity and adversity in almsgiving, and restrain their rage, and pardon the offenses of their fellowmen; and God loves the good-doers."[54] "O believers, among your wives and children there is an enemy to you; so beware of them. But if you pardon, and overlook, and if you forgive, surely God is All-forgiving, All-compassionate."[55] **Exception:** Do not forgive any attack on the religion of Islam or anyone who drives you from your homes. "It may be that Allah will grant love (and friendship) between you and those whom you (now) hold as enemies. For Allah has power (over all things); and Allah is Oft-Forgiving, Most Merciful. Allah does not forbid you, with regard to those who do not fight you for (your) Faith nor drive you out of your homes, from dealing kindly and justly with them: for Allah loves those who are just. Allah only forbids you, with regard to those who fight you for (your) Faith, and drive you out of your homes, and support (others) in driving you out, from turning to them (for friendship and protection). It is such as turn to them (in these circumstances), that do wrong."[56]

Acceptance of Forgiveness by Perpetrator

If the perpetrator acknowledges his or her wrongdoing, forgiveness is usually easier. Doing so assures the victim that the perpetrator is not likely to repeat the injury. However, it is possible to forgive even if the perpetrator is unwilling to acknowledge his/her misdeeds. The victim is freed from his/her burden and preoccupation of resentment by forgiving. Nevertheless, the victim may remain concerned and anxious about the perpetrator repeating the hurtful action.

Social Justice and Forgiveness in South Africa[57]

The dismantling of Apartheid is a wonderful story of farsightedness, courage, giving up of privileges, and forgiveness. Since colonial times, Apartheid had segregated South African citizens on the basis of skin color and ethnic origin: white, black, colored (mixed races), and Indian. This classification determined where they could live, which jobs were open to them, and what level of education was available to them. Over the years, killings, torture, kidnappings, disappearances, bombings, and massacres grew commonplace, both to support and to protest the system. Many of the atrocities were committed by the white police or security forces.

The white Afrikaners increasingly used the threat of communism as an excuse for maintaining Apartheid. When communism fell in 1989, that was no longer a credible excuse. State President F.W. de Klerk recognized that there could be no peace as long as some citizens were demeaned and denied common rights. There was general recognition that without a transfer of power the fighting and killings would intensify and spread. F.W. de Klerk led the National Party—which held the reigns of power—to support moving toward democracy. Still, many feared "paybacks" from one side to the other, which might result in years, if not centuries, of guerilla civil war. F.W. de Klerk spoke of power sharing. His political party freed prisoners, including African National Congress leader Nelson Mandela, who spent 27 years as a political prisoner. His suffering and jail time lent him authority and credibility.

Blacks, whites, colored, and Indians all wanted change. They wanted a stop to bombing and massacres. They wanted safety and security. In time, they wrote a new and liberal constitution. On April 27, 1994, they elected Nelson Mandela president. He was forgiving and conciliatory. At his inauguration, he invited his white jailor to be his honored guest.

The newly elected officials considered how government should deal with atrocities of the past. They rejected the model of the Nuremberg trials as too cumbersome, subject to subversion, divisive, and potentially traumatic for victims. Scarce funds to conduct the investigations and trials could be better used for housing, education, and medical care. Many records had been destroyed. Proof beyond reasonable doubt would be difficult. Further, the white security forces had all the weapons. On the other hand, granting blanket amnesty for everyone would disregard the victims' suffering, and a perceived lack of official concern would further dehumanize the victims.

The government instituted the Truth and Reconciliation Commission. Rather than prosecuting human-rights violators or granting blanket amnesty, it strengthened the attitude of forgiveness. Archbishop Desmond Tutu was appointed chair of the Commission. One of the main goals of the Commission was to treat victims with utmost respect and to prevent the experience from being traumatic or bewildering. "Our nation sought to rehabilitate and affirm the dignity and personhood of those who for so long had turned into anonymous marginalized ones. Now they would be able to tell their stories." They would be respected and acknowledged as equals.[58] As restorative justice, not retributive justice, this approach would strengthen the attitude of forgiveness.

People who applied for amnesty, which carried immunity from civil suits and damages, had to make full disclosure. The act(s) had to have occurred between 1960 and 1994. They had to have been politically motivated, not motivated by personal reasons. The rubric of proportionality had to be observed. Amnesty was not awarded to people who maintained innocence.

Another factor contributing to the peaceful transition was that most of the native leaders had attended Christian Church schools, where love and forgiveness were stressed. Archbishop Tutu also credits the native admiration for the personality traits of *Weltsanschauun*, or *ubuntu*. He describes such an individual as being generous, hospitable, friendly, caring, compassionate, and willing to share. "It is to say, 'My humanity is caught up, is inextricably bound up, in yours. We belong in a bundle of life.' We say, 'A person is a person through other persons.' ... It says, 'I am human because I belong, I participate, I share.' A person with *ubuntu* is open and available to others, affirming of others, does not feel threatened that others are able and good, for he or she has a proper self-assurance that comes from knowing that he or she belongs in a greater whole and is diminished when others are humiliated or diminished, when others are tortured or oppressed, or treated as if they were less than they are."[59]

Archbishop Tutu often said, "There can be no real peace (in the country) without forgiveness." Archbishop Tutu saw fit to include the reflections of Mrs. Marietta Jaeger on forgiveness of the man who abducted and murdered her seven-year-old daughter. The first portion of those reflections included:

> ... I had finally come to believe that real justice is not punishment but restoration, not necessarily to how things used to be, but to how they really should be. In both the Hebrew and Christian scriptures whence my beliefs and values come, the God who rises up from them is a God of mercy and compassion, a God who seeks not to punish, destroy, or put us to death, but a God who works unceasingly to help and heal us, rehabilitate and reconcile us, restore us to the richness and fullness of life for which we have been created. This, now, was the justice I wanted for this man who had taken my little girl.
>
> Though he was liable for the death penalty, I felt it would violate and profane the goodness, sweetness, and beauty of Susie's life by killing the kidnapper in her name. She was deserving of a more noble and beautiful memorial than a cold-blooded, premeditated, state-sanctioned killing of a restrained defenseless man, however deserving of death he may be deemed to be. I felt I far better honored her, not by becoming that which I deplored, but by saying that all life is sacred and worthy of preservation.[60]

Anarchy and the feared bloodbath were successfully averted. Three out-standing heroes brought this about: F.W. de Klerk, Nelson Mandela, and Arch-bishop Desmond Tutu, but the genuine heroes were the people themselves who recognized the wisdom of their leaders, gave up their privileges, and embraced forgiveness instead of revenge.

Conclusions

The missions of all religions call for similar actions rooted in love and compassion.

NOTES FOR CHAPTER FIVE

5.1   Das, Bhagavan: *The Essential Unity of All Religions*, Kessinger Pub Co, Kila, Montana, p. 297

5.2   Das, Bhagavan: cited, p. 302 & 325

5.3   Wattles, Jeffrey: *The Golden Rule*, Oxford University Press, New York, 1996, p. 4

5.4   Richards, Chris: *Illustrated Encyclopedia of World Religions*, Element Books, Inc, Rockport, Maine, 1997, p. 72

5.5   Wattles: p. 192

5.6   Wattles: p. 192

5.7   Wattles: p. 192

5.8   *Bible*: Leviticus 19:18

5.9   Wattles: p. 48

5.10 *Bible*: Matthew 7:12

5.11 *Bible*: Galatians 5:14

5.12 *Bible*: Romans 2:14-16

5.13 *Bible*: 1 John 4:20

5.14 Ibrahim, I.A., cited: *A Brief Illustrated Guide to Understanding Islam*, narrated in *Saheeh Al-Bukhari #13*, Darussalm Pub, Houston, Texas, 1997

5.15 Das, Bhagavan: *The Essential Unity of All Religions*; Muhammad in *Hadis Sithe*, Kissinger Pub Co, Kila, Montana, p. 298

5.16 Wattles: p. 192

5.17 Wattles: p. 192

5.18 Wattles: p. 193

5.19 Monroe, Charles R.: *World Religions, An Introduction*, Prometheus Books, Amherst, New York, 1995, p. 98

5.20 Monroe: p. 92

5.21 Monroe: p. 101

5.22 Monroe: p. 129

5.23 *Bible*: Leviticus 27:30 & 32

5.24 *Bible*: Malachi 3:10

5.25 Wuthnow, Robert: *After Heaven, Spirituality in America Since the 1950s*, University California Press, Berkley & Los Angeles, 1998, p. 3-4 & 39-40

5.26 Armstrong, Karen: *The History of God*, Alfred A. Knopf, New York, 1993, p. 48

5.27 *Bible*: 2 Corinthians 9:6-9

5.28 *Bible*: Matthew 6:2-4

5.29 *Bible*: Acts 10:1-2

5.30 Parrinder, Geoffrey, Editor: *World Religions*, Facts on File Publications, New York City, New York, 1985

5.31 Armstrong: p. 20

5.32 Monroe: p. 114

5.33 *Bible*: Amos 5:11-14

5.34 *Bible*: Amos Chapters 2-9

5.35 *Bible*: Jeremiah 22:13-17

5.36 *Bible*: Proverbs 14:31

5.37 *Qur'an*: 4:58

5.38 *Qur'an*: 4:49-9

5.39 *Qur'an*: 5:8, cited, Ibrahim, I.A.: *A Brief Illustrated Guide to Understanding Islam*, narrated in *Saheeh Al-Bukhari #13*, Darussalm Pub, Houston, Texas, 1997, p. 61-63

5.40 Tutu, Archbishop Desmond: *There Is No Future Without Forgiveness*, Doubleday, NYC, 1997, p. 54

5.41 Das: p. 311

5.42 Moses, Jeffrey: *Oneness, Great Principles Shared by All Religions*, Ballantine Books, Fawcett Columbine, New York, 1989, p. 75

5.43 Moses: p. 75

5.44 *Bible*: Leviticus 19:17-18

5.45 Waskow, Arthur: *Seasons of Our Joy, A Modern Guide to the Jewish Holidays,* Beacon Press, Boston, 1990, p. 3

5.46 Waskow: p. 8

5.47 Waskow: p. 31

5.48 Waskow: p. 39

5.49 Das: p. 309

5.50 *Bible*: Matthew 5:44

5.51 *Bible*: Matthew 6:12

5.52 *Bible*: Luke 11:4

5.53 *Bible*: Colossians 3:13-14

5.54 *Qur'an*, "The House of Imran," 12 7, Arberry, A.J., trans.: MacMillan Pub Co, NY 1955, p. 90

5.55 *Qur'an*, "Mutual Fraud," Arberry, A.J.: trans., MacMillan Pub Co, NY, 1955, p. 283

5.56 *Qur'an*, Al-Baqarah, Section 10:85

5.57 Tutu, Archbishop Desmond: *There Is No Future Without Forgiveness*, Doubleday, NYC, 1997

5.58 Tutu: p. 30

5.59 Tutu: p. 31

5.60 Tutu: p. 155-56

CHAPTER SIX

Spirituality

Supernatural Agency

Humans are inherently spiritual. Every society has believed in a supernatural force that could be influenced for the benefit of the individual or society. Attempts to ban spirituality by governments, such as those of the USSR and communistic China in the mid- and late-20th century, always inevitably fail to change what people believe. Every society has endeavored to communicate with that supernatural force or agent, which might be a grove of trees (the Druids), forces of nature (such as the sea or sexual attraction, as with the Greeks), ancestors (as the ancient Chinese and Australian aborigines), or the gods (as in ancient Greece and Rome).

Messages to the Supernatural

Messages to the supernatural from shamans, priests, prophets, and ordinary men and women have taken the forms of making sacrifices, praying, prostrating, conducting rituals, burning incense, lighting candles, tying written messages to sacred trees, painting with sand, painting rocks and caves, and invoking voodoo. Messages are also sent by living a religiously virtuous life, such as practicing The Golden Rule, giving alms, promoting social justice, and forgiving others' transgressions.

The spirits of ancestors are regarded by some peoples as supernatural agents. They are generally thought to have vested interests in their living descendents. They are believed to be able to influence lives in ways both beneficial and detrimental. People who embrace these beliefs generally take great pains to avoid angering their spirit ancestors, or to let them feel neglected. Some societies communicate directly with ancestors. This may involve a ritual, such as the North American Indian sweat-lodge ceremony.

Sacrifices needed to be of the best quality, not cull from the herd or blemished produce from the garden. The second Sutra of the *Qur'an* discusses the criteria for selecting a heifer for sacrifice. The *Bible* recounts how the king's sacrifice of his son on the city's wall motivated the Moab army, and made the Israelite army so fearful that they broke off the battle. Both sides expected the supernaturals would intervene.[1]

Whenever any spiritual ritual proves ineffective, a common explanation is that it was not performed correctly. In time, this results in some people specializing in the performance of rituals. These people become religious leaders, such as priests.

Messages from the Supernatural

Messages from the supernatural to humans have also taken many forms. The best-accepted of these are received by spiritual leaders—shamans, mystics, prophets, and others such as Saul on the road to Damascus.[2] Spirits of ancestors may communicate with messages, which are interpreted by the leaders, for most or all participants. Messages may be received from the heavens, such as through astrology or when the three wise men saw a star announcing the birth of Jesus.[3] Messages also may occur in the form of dreams, such as Jacob dreaming of a ladder to heaven,[4] or when Joseph was warned in a dream to flee with Mary and Jesus to Egypt.[5] Omens and oracles used to be common, such as reading the entrails of animals or tea leaves.[6]

Current events and unusual happenings have been interpreted by some as direct messages of divine intervention. Examples from the *Bible* include:

- The ten plagues against Egypt and the exodus from Egypt were believed to be the effect of God's direct intervention.[7]

- When Jonah refused to do the Lord's bidding, he tried to flee by ship, but a severe storm arose. The sailors were certain that the storm was sent by the Lord, so they drew lots to identify the culprit. The lot fell on Jonah.[8]

- Job's friends interpreted his loss of flocks and crops, his illnesses, and the deaths of his wife and children as a sure sign of God's punishment for Job's sins.[9]

Non-biblical examples include:

- The chief Roman god, Jupiter, who threw lightning bolts, was guardian of the city of Rome. When lightning destroyed his own temple and burned part of the city, it was interpreted as Jupiter being angry with the people of Rome. The people questioned what they had done that angered Jupiter.[10]

- The belief in God's direct intervention on the side of justice resulted in trials by combat in the Middle Ages in Europe.

- Often "yes" or "no" questions asked by humans have been "answered" by chance events such as which stall a cow entered in the barn.

After the exile of the Jews in 587 BCE, prophecy became the most dominant mode of communication from God for the Hebrews. Interpretation of current events/history remains a mode of receiving messages from God. Television evangelist Pat Robertson attributed the attacks on the World Trade Center buildings in New York City to American godlessness, e.g.: allowing abortion and "excluding God" from public schools. Sometimes the funerals of soldiers in the U.S. are picketed by a church that attributes such deaths to God's retribution for the "tolerance" of homosexuality.

Mysticism and Revelation

Man's inherent spirituality has long manifested itself many ways, especially through mystical experiences. There is often a loss of awareness of the self during a mystical experience. One of the universal themes of myths is the loss of a previous closeness or unity with God, or with the Ultimate. Many equate this with "the fall" of being cast out of the Garden of Eden, or being propelled by one's parents to leave the home and live independently. Later the sense of separateness arises from identifying the self with one's body.[11] There is an imperative to attempt to re-establish closeness.[12]

The goal of mystical experiences is to transcend the sense of individual self and to achieve a sense of wholeness and unity with God, the Ultimate, the Absolute, the Infinite. This is the state of *Unio Mystica*, or at a deeper level a state of *Absolute Unitary Being*, which is an ideal of mystics of monotheistic religions. This is also the Buddhist's loss of awareness of the self, which is Nirvana.

Mysticism has had many definitions. Tillich's definition of religious mysticism refers to inward participation in Ultimate Reality, or the Divine, through inner experience.[13] It may be induced by concentrating very intently on a religious image or concept and holding that focus. It may also come from looking deep within the self, essentially a spiritual activity. "True mystical achievement is the most complete and most difficult expression of life which is as yet possible to humans. It is at once an act of love, an act of surrender, and a supreme perception."[14] Without mysticism, only the thought aspects of religion remain, such as systems of ethics and doctrine. These statements can take on a supernatural aura, sometimes so strongly that they are never questioned. Theology derived from thought can be combined with theology taken from the feelings of inner experience. This is considered to create the highest experience of the

Divine Spirit, which, Tillich asserts, is the highest synthesis of what comes from the outside and what comes from the inside.[15] Tillich also asserts that the opposite of mysticism is not rationality, but rather theology demanded by religious authority.

The Mystic Experience

Transcendence is a crucial component of all mystical experience.[16] Denise and John Carmody (1995) defined a mystical experience as the direct experience of ultimate reality.[17] Usually a mystical experience begins by finding a place of solitude and quieting the mind. The mystic may try to enhance the experience by fasting, sleep deprivation, sensory deprivation, or use of plant extracts. The mystic may focus all his or her attention on an image, icon, or idea (usually culturally determined) that connotes intimacy with the Divine. Sometimes, there is a feeling of being outside of one's own body. Although it occurs rarely, this "out of body" experience may take place in response to beauty, pain, or a feeling so unfamiliar that one dissociates.

In 1911 Evelyn Underhill, a British scholar, published a magnum opus titled *Mysticism, the Nature and Development of Spiritual Consciousness.*[18] She explained that the goal of the mystic is a state of at-oneness with God—a complete union with the Absolute and nothing else. When achieved, this union is conscious, personal, and complete.[19] It is not theoretical. Mysticism is entirely a psychological, spiritual process of remaking consciousness.[20] The business and methods of mysticism are love.[21] Mysticism is never seeking self gain or the joys of the world as magic does. Rather, it is giving, not taking. Mysticism involves the whole self, not just thought. It is wholly transcendent and spiritual in aim, an action of the heart. It is a state in which the human mind transcends itself.[22] It is living in union with The One. "I live, yet not I, but God in me."

In a mystical experience, the individual often experiences a sense of being enfolded or engulfed by some force so powerful that it bypasses all intermediaries and leads directly to the Ultimate. It generates a sense of *union* or merger that reveals the legitimacy of the Divine to the mystic, of the process, of everything in the world. There is an absence of a sense of time and space, including past and future. The experience becomes alive, moving, commanding, and perhaps even threatening. Double or even contradictory feelings are not unusual. It glows in the mystics' hearts and minds. There is no doubt. It is totally compelling. Typically, it is not attributed to the effort or status of the mystic, but to being open to experiencing the Ultimate. The mystical experience may come spontaneously or by patterns of thought.[23] The Divine is often discovered in spiritual and mystical encounters.[24] In addition to a sense of joy and peace, mystical experiences relieve existential anxiety and engender a sense of safety in an uncertain and often terrifying world. They give hope, and thereby helped the human race to survive.[25] Many great concepts of all major religions have been discovered during experiences with spiritual and mystical reality.[26]

Mysticism in All Cultures

Mysticism is thought to be at least similar, if not the same, in all religions and through the centuries. Evelyn Underhill studied the lives of mystics of both the East and West, including their writings and autobiographies, as well as what others had written about them. Published in 1911, her book contains an appendix of all the known Christian mystics through Blake. She stated that the aims, doctrines, and methods of mystics have been substantially the same, regardless of the place or period in which the mystic lived.[27] A Hindu mystic is thought to have essentially the same experience as the Jewish, Christian, or aboriginal Australian mystics.[28]

The mystics describe their experiences of the Ultimate using their own and their audience's symbols and terms such as God or Allah, or the ideal states of Tao or Nirvana. Symbolism is always used to explain spiritual and mystic life.[29] Whatever the description, it may seem so inadequate to the mystic that s/he may feel that having no description at all would be closer to the truth. Were it not for the speaker's deep sincerity, listeners might think the mystic is playing a word game rather than attempting to describe the indescribable. Generally, the mystic readily acknowledges that s/he has seen only a part, but that part represents the whole. The Hindu mystic often resorts to negative descriptions—"not this, not that." The Taoist holds the conviction that those who speak do not know. For the Buddhist, the difference of everyday opposites collapses into a unified sameness.[30]

The Carmodys note that the mystic usually feels a compelling certainty about the disclosure, but feels unsure and inadequate in his/her attempts to describe the experience.[31] If the mystic expresses confidence in his or her description of what happened and the communication means, it raises serious doubt as to whether or not the mystical experience really happened.

Mystic Communication from God

Probably the least understood aspects of mysticism are the forms of communication the mystic receives from God. Underhill declares that God speaks to people from the subconscious, which means that impressions of the Eternal are intuitions rather than rational thoughts.[32] It is a picture which the subconscious constructs from raw material already in each person's mind. Visions and voices are considered to be related to the mystics in ways similar to how paintings, poems, and musical compositions are to their creators. Mystic compositions may be more meaningful than reality in terms of truth, beauty, or life. They are messages from the deeper subconscious mind to the surface mind. These automatisms may be received as auditions, visions, or automatic writing. Each of these may occur in any of three modes: instant internal, distinct internal, and distinct external.

Auditions

For auditions the inarticulate *instant internal* voice may occur in an instant of time—a whole message is suddenly received. Mystics prefer the inarticulate mode of communication. St. Hildagarde received her communication instantly.[33] This is similar if not identical to the way Wolfgang Mozart heard music.

> Whence and how these things come I know not, nor can I force them… Nor do I hear in my imagination the parts successively, but I hear them all the same.
>
> —Wolfgang Mozart[34]

A second mode is the *distinct internal* voice, perfectly articulate. It speaks only within the mind, such as what we experience in dreams during sleep.

The first two modes are somewhat analogous to the ways a person may read. A rapid reader absorbs information from the page without his mind forming each word in thought. Comprehension is often just as great as that of the slow reader who forms each word mentally.

The third mode is the *distinct external* voice. It is experienced as though heard by the ear.

Underhill reports that mystics are unanimous in their preference that the inarticulate voice is most trustworthy. The other two modes are somewhat suspect of containing some degree of distortion or illusion. She quotes St. Ambrose: "Let Thy good Spirit enter my heart and there be heard without utterance, and without the sound of words speak all truth."[35] She cites two other saints who report that they received lengthy communications from God in an instant of time.

With articulated words, internally or externally, there is a need for the communication to be scrutinized and evaluated carefully to determine whether or not it is from God. True auditions are usually heard without conscious thought, when the mind is in a state of deep absorption. However, some saints have heard messages from God by articulated words either inside the head or by the ear.[36] Moses heard the voice of God speaking to him from a burning bush.[37] Dialogues with the Divine have also been reported by some mystics. This is somewhat similar to the common phenomenon of arguing with one's self. Often the words are thought or heard. It is the divine voice from the mystic's subconscious to the mystic's conscious mind. Auditions often have a rhythmic or exalted character similar to poetry. The beauty of the *Qur'an* in Arabic is a classic example. These phenomena may also occur with automated writing.

Visions

Mystics tend to be very skeptical of visions. They are believed more likely to occur as a result of distortions, optical illusions, or an intoxicating substance than are auditory illusions or hallucinations. Visions are divided into the same three modes, and further distinguished as *passive* or *active*. Passive visions are not sought, but rather appear before the mind.

Visions do not have to be distinct. They can be perceived by the whole self as neither sight nor feeling, or with parts of both. They are definite, yet impossible to define. They are often interpreted as a consciousness of the presence of God. They can be located in space, even though not seen with the eyes. These visions may be instant, or they may last for days.[38] There are no forms to be seen, yet there is certainty of the visions that is more certain than seeing. Passive imaginary visions are always internal. They are expressions of thought, desire, or perception of the deeper self. They are described as similar to Wordsworth's "dancing daffodils." Active imaginary visions are expressions of changes in the self. They are a visible sign of movement toward new levels of consciousness for the mystic.[39]

Automatic Writing

Automatic writing may manifest itself as a compulsion to write. In the most intense form one's hand seems to become the agent of another personality. Evelyn Underhill described the automatic writing of St. Catherine of Siena: "The writing is entirely characteristic of subliminal energy of a rich type, dissociated from the criticism and control of normal consciousness, in that its loose employment of metaphor, the strangely mingled intimacy and remoteness of its tone link it with prophetic literature."[40] Automatic writing is usually swift, without hesitations or modifications. That is, these thoughts emerge from the subconscious mind into awareness. They contain a higher percentage of symbols than occur in daily thinking. This type of thinking is called primary-process thinking.

Other Evidence for Spirituality

What is considered a virtuous life is similar in all religions. Also similar are the emotional responses to a personal encounter with the Holy. This has been found to be essentially the same in all parts of the world, and judging from descriptions in sacred scripture, the reaction has been the same throughout history.[41] These mystical experiences occur over a wide range of societies, from advanced industrial and informational ones to primitive ones with their reverence for nature, ancestors, and the shaman.

Aristotle noted that people initiated into one of the mystery religions of Greece were not required to learn new facts or to adopt a creed or espouse a doctrine, but rather to experience certain emotions and be put in a certain disposition. This observation gave rise to the theory that tragedy effected a catharsis of the emotions of terror and pity that amounted to a rebirth. Greek tragedies were originally part of the religious festivals, and were attempting to reveal fundamental and universal truths through poetic expressions.[42]

Additional evidence that spirituality is inherent within humans consists of the whole ontological argument of Plato's transcendent truths, which hold that anyone has the potential to find universal transcendent values by looking deeply within the self. The mystical experiences described by Denise and John Carmody contain essentially the same elements worldwide throughout history.

In these universal mystical states sacred insights are often first discovered and/or revealed. Although a mystic is aware that he or she has seen only a part, the mystic's followers are so eager to hold on to the transcendent message(s) that they often confuse the finite ethnic aspects with the infinite aspects. They do not realize that the mystic has been only a part. The followers, both the contemporaries of the mystic as well as those of later generations, don't have the hesitation of the mystic. The followers want more. They want answers.

They want an entire system.

NOTES FOR CHAPTER SIX

6.1   *Bible*: 2 Kings 3:5-27

6.2   *Bible*: Acts 9:3

6.3   *Bible*: Matthew 2:1

6.4   *Bible*: Genesis 28:12

6.5   *Bible*: Matthew 2:13

6.6   Mann, Charles: *1491: New Revelations of the Americas Before Columbus*, Alfred A. Knopf Pub., New York, 2005, p. 78 & 239

6.7   *Bible*: Exodus 7:8-12:36

6.8   *Bible*: Jonah 1-4

6.9   *Bible*: Job 3-31

6.10 Holland, Tom: *Rubicon, the Last Years of the Roman Empire*, Doubleday, New York City, 2003, p. 82

6.11 Newberg, Andrew, M.D.; d'Aquili, Eugene, M.D., PhD; Rause, Vince: *Why God Won't Go Away*, Ballantine Books, New York City, 2001, p. 103

6.12 Newberg: p. 91; & Armstrong, Karen: *A Short History of Myth*, Conongate, New York City, 2005, p. 14

6.13 Tillich, Paul: *A History of Christian Thought*, Touchstone Books, Simon & Schuster, New York, 1967, p. 318

6.14 Underhill, Evelyn: *Mysticism, the Nature and Development of Spiritual Consciousness*, Oneworld Publications, Oxford, England, 1999, p. 84

6.15 Tillich: p. 317

6.16 Carmody, Denise & John: *Mysticism*, Oxford University Press, Oxford and New York, 1996, p. 8-9

6.17 Carmody: p. 10

6.18 Underhill: p. 72

6.19 See Chapter Seven, "Studying the Brain"

6.20 Underhill: p. 84

6.21 Newberg: p. 174

6.22 Armstrong, Karen: *A Short History of Myth*, Canongate, New York City, 2005, p. 8

6.23 Newberg: p. 134

6.24 Newberg: p. 133

6.25 Newberg: p. 131

6.26 Newberg: p. 135

6.27 Underhill: p. 3

6.28 Carmody: p. 9

6.29 Underhill: p. 19 & 21

6.30 Carmody: p. 6

6.31 Carmody: p. 9

6.32 Underhill: p. 52

6.33 Underhill: p. 273

6.34 Underhill: p. 277

6.35 Underhill: p. 274

6.36 Underhill: p. 275

6.37 *Bible*: Exodus 3:3-9

6.38 Underhill: p. 294

6.39 Armstrong: p. 37

6.40 Underhill: p. 294

6.41 See Chapter Two

6.42 Armstrong: p. 99

CHAPTER SEVEN

Biological Evidence
For "Built-in Spirituality"

Every function of the mind has its physiological basis in the brain. This includes every perception, emotion, thought, and voluntary action; every image, fantasy, and dream; and everything an individual knows, whether cognitively or intuitively. Every experience, such as feelings of transcendence, feelings of numinousness, all beliefs, all values, and all mystical states of absolute unity with the Divine take place in the brain. All awareness happens in the substrate of the brain, as does all analysis, including analysis of the nervous system itself.

The Human Nervous System

The nervous system is composed of nerve cells. Each cell has an input side and an output side. Between these two sides is the cell body, which contains the nucleus. Except in the autonomic nervous system, all nerve cell bodies are inside the skull or in the spinal cord. Nerve endings on the input side have various transducers that trigger nerve impulses. A transducer converts one form of energy into a different form. The retina of the eye converts light energy into electrical energy that gets sent to the brain. Similarly, the cochlear of the ear changes sound waves to electrical energy. Both pressure on the skin and pain are converted to electrical energy. There are only two modes of communication within the Central Nervous System: nerve impulses (electrical) and hormones (chemical). All messages must be converted into one of these energy systems. One nerve cell may be connected to multiple transducers, always of the same type. All perceptions originate on the input side of a nerve cell.

The output side may go either to a muscle, to a gland that secretes a hormone, or to other nerve cells for information processing, including memory storage or retrieval. Nerves often occur in groups or clusters to coordinate neural responses or to facilitate information processing. In the brain, some of these clusters have names that reflect their function. Structures identified before their function was known tend to have names (usually in Latin) reflecting their appearance or their locale, or they may be named after the scientific pioneer who described them.

Inside the brain there are three large divisions as to appearance, evolutionary development, and function. They are the *brain stem,* the *limbic system,* and the *neocortex.*

The Brain Stem

Often called the *reptilian brain,* the brain stem controls breathing, swallowing, heart rate, visual tracking, a startle center, thirst, movement, aggression, territorial defense, "freezing," avoidance and withdrawal, and mating behavior patterns. The brain stem in humans may continue to function even when the other two parts of the brain do not function, a state referred to as "brain dead." In popular fiction, "zombies" are typically depicted as human corpses with the reptilian parts of their brains reactivated.

The Limbic System

The *limbic system* first appeared in the evolution of mammals. The limbic brain is the seat of most emotions and the memories associated with emotions. It evaluates external inputs as well as inputs from the body for their emotional relevance.[1] The limbic system enables a person to interpret the emotional nuances of another's speech, and to imbed emotional nuances in one's own verbalizations. People can read even fleeting emotions displayed by human faces, including newborns and infants. The limbic brain is the neurological origin of dreams. The limbic system also receives inputs from the neocortex centers that appraise value.

Without the limbic system there is no personality. If the limbic system is destroyed in an experimental animal, that animal reacts as if others do not exist. The experimental animal is apt to climb on another as if climbing on rocks.

On the input side, the limbic system receives relays of all emotional messages. Mammals can detect the emotional state of other mammals and adjust their own responses, e.g.: a dog will know whether a human is afraid of him. When a pet owner is distraught or depressed, it is not unusual for the pet to go to the owner with concern and perhaps to offer comfort. Called limbic resonance, this awareness also includes the mutual recognition of sexual interest between two potential lovers who have just met. Two mammals can also become attuned to each other's or the group's internal state. Women who spend a lot of time with one another may find their menstrual cycles coming into spontaneous alignment.

Limbic resonance occurs between mother and newborn infant, and is responsible for attachment attitudes and behaviors. Close synergism between mother and infant results in the infant's confidence in him/herself, in the mother, and in the world. In situations that are novel, the child will look to the mother for cues as to emotional meaning. Disruption of limbic resonance and its attachment results in protest and, if prolonged, in despair. Released in the mother's brain during delivery, "attachment hormone" oxytocin greatly facilitates bonding. Oxytocin is also released in both genders at puberty and with sexual orgasm.

In the 13th century and again in the 1940s, groups of infants were subjected to special circumstances: all of their physical needs were met promptly, but they were not talked to or played with. All the infants in the earlier group died. The 1940s infants were housed in different cities and had different staff. 75-99% of the children in each institution died. Communicated love alters the structure of brains. A person cannot know the self without someone else knowing him. Limbic resonance is responsible for the phenomena of group psychology and emotional contagion. Who we become is determined in large part by whom we love and by who loves us. Loss of attachment such as rejection by a sweetheart or the death of a loved one results in grief and depression. Ostracism and banishment are painful punishments precisely because they disrupt attachment.

Learning in the limbic system may occur implicitly, i.e.: without conscious awareness. This emotional learning begins at birth, if not earlier. The limbic system makes an emotional model of specific relationships, of relationships in general, and of the world. These *patterns* are strengthened with use in life and in fantasy.[2]

The limbic system itself does not distinguish between happenings in the real world and in fantasy. That is why an individual may enjoy (or experience fear or other emotions) reading a novel, watching a movie, or simply fantasizing. This same mechanism allows trying scenarios in thought to see how emotions would feel if they occurred in real life.

The limbic system has significant survival advantages. It is responsible for the aggression needed to find and defend food. It alerts the mammal to dangerous situations with fear, and it drives the desire to mate. The limbic system contains the hypothalamus, which acts as the master controller of the autonomic nervous system, which has two divisions. The *parasympathetic*—or quiescent—division handles the "housekeeping." The *sympathetic* division is responsible for arousal, the "fight or flight" response, and fear responses. The limbic system can trigger *thought* and *action*, but it is the very seat of all feeling.

Understanding Some Deep Religious Experiences Neurologically

The common experiences given below differ from some deep religious experiences only in intensity. Brain studies illustrate the neurophysiology.

Consider the experiences of a person becoming "lost" in a good book to the extent that it holds one's full attention. This results in:

- a decrease in the awareness that time is passing
- a decrease in awareness of inputs from the environment
- a loss of the sense of self
- an identification with the most prominent character in the book
- experiencing the same type(s) of emotions that are portrayed for the main character of the book

In general, the deeper the concentration, the greater are the effects mentioned above. These circumstances may occur while listening to music or while struggling toward the solution of a mechanical/engineering problem, as well as reading a book.

Now suppose that, instead of on a book, the individual concentrates just as intently on God or on a religious concept. Here, too, there is the lack of awareness of time, a marked decrease of awareness of environmental inputs, a decrease in the sense of self, and identification with the subject of concentration—in this case God. Further, consider that this concentration continues for long periods of time and is repeated frequently. These same phenomena occur during brain scans and in other research situations.

Mystical experiences generally begin as an act of will, by either "emptying the mind of all thought"—the *passive approach*—or by focusing one's attention intently on a thought, a mantra, an icon, a lighted candle, or an image, perhaps the image or thought of God, the *active approach*. Alternatively, one may begin by becoming absorbed in what one is doing (action), such as fighting, defiantly standing, singing, or suffering physical pain.

When maximal arousal breaks through the quieting responses of the *hypothalamus*, chief controller of the autonomic nervous system, it causes total suppression of input, which results in loss of ego boundaries and an absolute sense of unity with the whole world—or with what might be perceived as Good. This is the *Unio Mysterica*, the Christian mystic's mystical union with God; it is also the

Buddhist's Ultimate, the state of emptiness. These are not two different mental mechanisms, nor can there be two different philosophical versions of the *Unio Mysterica*. Rather, these differences are in the interpretation of the experience.

Perhaps the most beneficial survival functions of the mind is its automatic, omnipresent, and compulsive drive to make a holistic concept of the world— of all its perceptions and experiences, including the past experiences, teachings, understandings, and beliefs. Such integration is necessary for the mystic to explain the phenomena to him/herself and to comrades who share similar background. This need to integrate experiences and to make sense of the world is one of the major cognitive functions of the mind.

Newberg and d'Aquili hold that the realization of the Divine comes to humans in a mystical or spiritual experience through neurological processes. The Divine is interpreted as real because it is experienced. The sense of self has been transcended, and the experience is "good." Even much milder forms of mystical experiences, such as falling in love, leave no room for doubt. They are genuine! Mystical experiences can be sought, or they may come to those who do not seek them, just as falling in love may occur spontaneously and unexpectedly, possibly even when the experience is not desired.

Myths

The human mind's compulsion to make an understandable model of the world is continuous, and is used in regard to all types of situations. Remember, the greater the anxiety and the need to comprehend, the greater the urge to create a coherent concept. When the issue is existential, the solution is apt to be mythical.[3]

A myth is defined here as a story that may be accurate and historically true, or it may be a fabrication. Myths are stories that reconcile two seemingly contradictory sets of facts or suppositions, either of an existential nature, or of the individual or the society. The power of a myth is not in its literal interpretation of the story, but rather in its symbols and metaphors. It speaks from the right side of the brain, more as intuition than logic. It speaks of psychological and spiritual truths. By this definition all religions are founded on myths. Otherwise, the religions would not be perceived to have any meaningful messages for humanity. Newberg points out that Joseph Campbell and other scholars of myths recognize that many myths from varying cultures and across time deal with very similar themes. Further, they stress that the evolutionary function of these neurological operators is to enhance survival, not to establish truth.

Any existential idea might become a myth if it can unify the logic of the left hemisphere and intuition of the right, thereby achieving whole-brain harmony. The sharing of this experience with others will be accepted by many because they, too, see the analogy, and because of the leader's conviction and its emotional contagion. By this limbic resonance, they share the leader's emotional experience and certainty. They believe it because they experience the same certainty as does the leader. A myth is born, a myth that may well bolster, enhance, or add new facets to a religion—or become the basis of founding a new one.

NOTES FOR CHAPTER SEVEN

7.1   Lewis, Thomas, M.D.; Amini, Fari, M.D.; Lennon, Richard, M.D: *A General Theory of Love*, Vintage Books, Div of Random House, Inc., New York City, 2000

7.2   Newberg, Andrew, M.D.; d'Aquili, Eugene, M.D.; Rause, Vince: *Why God Won't Go Away*, Ballantine Books, New York City, 2001

7.3   See Chapter One, "Integration Difficulties" & Chapter Three, "Myths"

CHAPTER EIGHT

Changing Views of the World

One of the major functions of religion throughout the centuries has been to provide tentative answers to life's existential questions—the questions of existence. These include: Why are things as they are? What is the purpose of life, of my life? Where was I before I was born? What happens after death? Is there order in the universe? What is the cause and purpose of tragedy?

Most religions have proposed answers—often stringing them together to make a system. These early questions may well have been related to the issue of order vs. chaos. As stated earlier, the Aztecs believed that human help was essential to maintain order in the world. The myth of Demeter and Persephone gave the Greeks an explanation of the seasons. The heavens were orderly, as were the seasons.

Dean Kelly of the National Council of Churches stated, "Humans are inveterate meaning-mongers. Humans try to make sense out of their experiences, even if they have to use nonsense to do so." Humans intrinsically look for patterns, even when there are none, as the Greeks and Romans did by grouping stars into constellations representing figures of animals and humans.[1]

Kelly stated that one of the main functions of religion is to provide meaning for life, regardless of how partial, incomplete, or even nonsensical the explanations. The answers to existential questions involve connections to, and a relationship with, the Divine.[2]

These existential questions are universal, but the ways humans have devised to deal with them are exceedingly diverse, which in turn generate a plethora of beliefs and religions. One faith may help integrate its society by preaching brotherly love; another may help integration by preaching a holy war against others. Examples of the latter include the Crusades, the Inquisition, and jihad.[3] Both kinds of integration explain the meaning of life to their followers.[4] The answers themselves are often less important than the fact that presumed answers are presented. When society changes so much that the answers are no longer satisfactory, the religion falters. Without some system of answers or beliefs and practices to deal with these issues, life may be experienced as empty—meaningless. In his classic study of suicide, Emile Durkhein called this malady *anomie (anomy)*.[5] The ultimate terror of life is meaninglessness!

Intrigued by world mythologies all his life, Joseph Campbell identified four functions that are indispensable for people to make sense of the world and our place in it:

- **The metaphysical function,** which opens up peoples' awareness that under the surface there is a transcendent, a mystery source, that is the same force that is within yourself, the awareness and appreciation of the metaphysical—the spiritual.[6]

- **The cosmological function,** which is the popular image of the world and the cosmos. This image has changed radically over the centuries. For metaphysical beliefs to be effective they must be compatible with the current, popular, accepted view of the cosmos. In ancient times the worldview consisted of what was visible, from where the sun rose in the East and moved to where it set in the West. Copernicus and Kepler showed this concept to be incorrect, that the world's rotation produces days and nights.

- **The pedagogical function,** which guides each individual and his guardians harmoniously through the inevitable crises in every stage of life—babyhood, childhood, adolescence, becoming accepted as an adult, working, marriage and bearing children, illnesses and injuries, old age, and the illnesses and deaths of others who are close.

- **The sociological function,** which validates and maintains specific social order in society here and now.[7]

Paul Tillich said that because societies are constantly undergoing change, some of their religious symbols may lose their prior meaning and thus their redemptive power.[8] It is not that the Ultimate has changed; rather, it is human understanding that has changed. All religious symbols are of this world—that is, they are finite—but to be meaningful, symbols must be transparent to the Infinite. A continuous search for more meaningful symbols with the deepest and clearest transparency to the Ultimate is absolutely necessary to preserve the vitality of a religion.[9] When symbols lose their spiritual meaning, they cannot be revived, although some may be reinterpreted. New transparent symbols cannot be simply created. They can only be discovered in the sense of being recognized. They grasp us.[10] The criterion is always: Does the Ultimate shine through the finite or not?

Some Changes Since 1941

Consider how events during and after WWII were interpreted to satisfy the four functions identified by Joseph Campbell. Much of what happened both strengthened and challenged established assumptions about the world and about American life, including religious life. WWII was seen as inevitable just after the attack on Pearl Harbor. Most American religious leaders supported the war. Seminaries trained clergy for the military. The goals of the government and those of mainstream Christianity were allied, to defeat the "evil" regimes of Nazi Germany and Japan. For many this perception continued after the war; they interpreted the outcomes as God supporting the allies. During the late 1940s and '50s, seminaries overflowed with students seeking deeper religious insights. Many stayed in the ministry.

Some people gave WWII's events different interpretations. The old philosophical problem of evil re-emerged:

- The death-camp murders of eleven-million people by one nation, many of them citizens of its own country, raised the "problem of the existence of evil in the world" to a new level. Five million were killed for reasons ranging from culture to sexuality, behavior, politics, and physical or mental disability. However, six million were killed only because of their religion, Judaism. This caused some people to question both the fairness and the protection of God.

- Many people lost family members in the war despite their frequent fervent prayers for their relatives' safe return.

- There were 298,000 American casualties, 18 million casualties in the Soviet Union, and a grand total of 37,468,000 casualties worldwide.[11]

- The extent of the suffering caused by the death and displacement of civilians, as well as destruction of property, added extra weight to the question of evil in the world.

How could an all-powerful God allow all this to happen? He had intervened in human affairs on the side of justice before. Why not this time in the face of such evil and such suffering?

- The Soviet Union and China outlawed all religions, which challenged some people's assumptions of the ultimate predominance of religion.

However, religion did re-emerge in these countries as soon as repression was lifted. Religion had merely gone underground.

- More than ever before, the American servicemen and women had greater contact with people of other religions. Many realized that other religious systems were also effective for their adherents.

- A large number of American veterans took advantage of educational opportunities under the GI Bill of Rights. Many learned that different cultural and religious systems could serve the needs of people like themselves. Many examined their own religions in light of their new knowledge.

The last time anything comparable happened on such a scale was during the Crusades when Europeans learned of the scientific superiority of Islamic countries. A major result in Europe was a marked turning toward science, philosophy, and theology, which helped foster the Renaissance in learning, letters, and art; then later led to the Reformation.

After the war, more revelations followed:

- The atomic and hydrogen bombs gave people a different perspective on the world and the role of humans in it.

- The introduction of safe, effective, and easy-to-use methods of contraception gave people greater control over biological functions long considered purviews of the Divine. By 1963, 2.3 million American women had decided for themselves to take birth-control pills.

- Putting men on the moon and exploring space gave most people a new concept of the vast universe. Some had trouble shifting from a literal heaven "up there" to a spiritual concept of heaven.

- The discovery of the Dead Sea Scrolls and the manuscripts of Nag Hammadi, combined with scholarship in related subjects, further opened up critical studies of the *Bible*.

- More progressive perspectives on prejudice and discrimination emerged. Women had moved into factory positions during the war and had done very well. After the war, some were not willing to be excluded from those jobs. The African Americans as a group had done well in every position they were allowed to enter. Many people recognized their own attitudes had been discriminatory, and therefore wrong. To the extent these prior attitudes were thought to have been supported by religion, religion was also called into question. It was a time to throw out many old beliefs.

- The assassination of President Kennedy made many Americans feel vulnerable, and reminded them that nations can be harmed by evil despite whatever protections religion is believed to offer.

- The Vietnam War's perceived inequity toward those who were drafted, the gross decrease in trust of the truthfulness of American leaders, and the post-war inflationary economic crisis created great disillusionment of our way of life.

- The country and the world became "smaller" as awareness of environmental pollution increased. For many, the calling of human beings was no longer to exploit nature, but rather to respect and preserve it.

- The mobility of people in pursuit of work, education, recreation, and health care reduced the sanctity once associated with a particular place: nation, town, home, job, school, or place of worship.

These events caused changes in each of Campbell's categories. There was a new and deeper realization that the world and even the universe are just as potentially subject to human intervention and manipulation as ordinary things are. With various lag times, people question themselves, their nation, their place in the world, and their religions and beliefs.

Religions Do Change

Changes often come slowly and tentatively, including reversals. The roots of a change may go back centuries. One major religious change with these characteristics occurred in Judaism. Reform and Conservative synagogues began leaving the traditions of Orthodox synagogues' ways of living. One document in the United States that called for Jewish worship choices was called the Pittsburgh Platform:

> Today we accept as binding only its moral laws and maintain only such ceremonials as elevate and sanctify our lives, but reject all such as are not adapted to the views and habits of modern civilization.
>
> We hold that all such Mosaic and Rabbinical laws as regulate diet, priestly purity and dress originated in ages and under the influence of ideas altogether foreign to our present mental and spiritual state.

We recognize Judaism as a progressive religion, ever striving to be in accord with the postulates of reason.[12]

The Roman Catholic Church held Vatican II in the last half of the 20th century. They sanctioned local languages for use in the mass, replacing traditional Latin only. They had the priest turn around to face the congregation. They modified much of their liturgy in a document called the Liturgy Constitution.[12]

At the close of the 2nd session of Vatican II, December 4, 1962, Pope John Paul II stated in part, "If, at this juncture, we have set out to simplify the external expression of worship, in an effort to make it more comprehensible to our people and closer to current speech, this does not mean that we wish to reduce the importance of prayer, or to put it on a lower plane than other obligations of the sacred ministry or of the apostolate. Neither does it mean that we want to make worship less expressive or less esthetically satisfying. It is rather that we want to make it purer, more genuine, closer to the sources of truth and grace, better fitted to be the spiritual patrimony of the people."

After many centuries of the Catholic Church denouncing advances in scientific study, such as condemning new astronomical models of our solar system and the universe, Pope John Paul II surprised many by declaring that the Church accepts current theories about evolution and origin of species.

Both the Catholic Church and the Mormons still forbid birth control, but many women and couples of these religions choose to use it, and many strongly advocate changing this policy. What positions to take about the right to choose abortion is a major issue in many Protestant denominations. Ordination of women, gays, and lesbians is controversial. Some churches may well splinter over these issues.

Buddhism provides another example of religion adapting to change. Many Buddhists in the United States are working to shift their worship services designed for monastery settings to other forms that are better adapted to daily life. Islamic countries face the difficult decisions about how to express Islamic culture, especially of Sharia-based laws—and if so, what to set as the punishment for violations.

Many conservative churches stress the ultimate concern of most of the people in their congregations to the existential question, "Is there individual existence after death?" The answer of the conservative churches is an emphatic, "Yes, each individual will spend all eternity blissfully in heaven or tormented in hell." This answer has implications for two other existential questions: "What is the purpose of life?" and "How should I live my life?" Many churches hold that the purpose of life is a test, a trial to determine where one will spend eternity. There is nothing more important to conservative Christians who hold these beliefs. Their religion prescribes how one is to live life to guarantee a place in heaven. The simple biblical answer is belief in God: "For God so loved the world that he gave his only Son, so that everyone who believes in him may not perish but may have eternal life."[13] This answer extends to both the feeling of love toward God and loving action to others. Not to live such a life is interpreted as not really believing. If s/he really did believe, s/he would live the religious life.

The value of salvation is supported by the commitment of the leaders and by the followers. "You can be saved. You can make a difference." People need to be a part of something greater than themselves. These churches emphasize recruiting people from the least advantaged strata of society, people who have rarely experienced others valuing them and asking for their help. The value of joining equals the cost of commitment. If the cost is little, the natural assumption is that joining cannot be worth much. The greater the cost, the greater the implied worth, and the greater the desirability of belonging.[14]

Kelly said, "The quality that enables religious meanings to take hold is not their rationality, their logic, their surface credibility, but rather the *demand* they make upon their adherents and the degree to which that demand is met by *commitment*."[15] Kelly demonstrates the validity of these statements by examples of the early Christians, the Anabaptists, and the Wesleyans, as well as the Mormons and the Jehovah's Witnesses.[16] The signers of the U.S. Declaration of Independence understood the costs of commitment. The sentence just above their signatures reads, "With a firm reliance on the protection of Divine Providence, we mutually pledge to each other our Lives, our Fortunes, and our Sacred Honor." Also, Jesus said, "If any man would come after me let him deny himself and take up his cross and follow me."[17]

Martin Luther King, Jr., preached brotherly love, and that one's conscience speaks authoritatively regardless of external interventions. He urged people to make their own decisions about what is right and wrong. This was freedom of choice based on freedom of conscience. During that time, many questioned the government's interpretation of the meaning of the Vietnam War, the wisdom of the government's decisions, and the fairness of the draft—even the government's right of conscription. Many young men and their families who rebelled against government authority also began to leave the mainline churches and religions, often turning instead to spirituality.[18]

Change Is Inevitable

Historically significant events will always change societies and compel people to adapt. This includes changes in religion, whether by adapting for all adherents or splintering to meet the needs of whatever portion demands change. While changes within long-established religions tend to occur slowly, history shows that some have managed to adapt quickly. This willingness to embrace change has proven a powerful contributor to their success in attracting and holding new generations of congregations.

Many parts of the world, especially those with expanding information technology, are experiencing increasingly rapid exposure to varying cultures, disparate ideas, and greater understanding of scientific answers to questions long considered the purview of religion. This puts ever more pressure on religions to address many new ways of thinking.

Researchers in the United States have been reporting a decline in church affiliation, but closer examination often reveals the decrease to be mostly in identifying with an organized religion, not a waning belief in God or some form of spirituality. Churches that adapt to a diversity of ideas, and which focus on social justice and loving consideration of others, are growing in popularity.

We live in an era when people of all faiths and no faith are routinely being exposed to others' cultures and religious beliefs. Many will find ways to accommodate our differences in a spirit of harmony. This is the greatest challenge all religions face today. Since change is inevitable, we might as well drive that change for the best. How religions adapt to a changing world will profoundly affect us all.

NOTES FOR CHAPTER EIGHT

8.1   See Chapter Three, Spirituality"

8.2   Campbell, Joseph: Mythos 1.1

8.3   See Chapter Nine, "Responses"

8.4   Brown, D. MacKenzie: *Ultimate Concern, Tillich in Dialogues*, Harper and Row, New York City, 1965, p. 3

8.5   Brown: p. 90

8.6   Goetz, Philip, Editor in chief: *New Encyclopaedia Britannica*, 15th Ed, Vol 29, Encyclopaedia Britannica, Inc., 1990, p.1023

8.7   Kelley, Dean: *Why Conservative Churches Are Growing*, Harper and Row, New York, 1972, p. 38

8.8   Kelley: p. 30

8.9   Kelley: p. 51+

8.10 Stark, Rodney, cited: *The Rise of Christianity*, Harper, San Francisco, 1996, p. 53

8.11 *The Liturgy Constitution*, Deus Books, Paulist Press, Glen Rock, NJ, 1964

8.12 John Paul II: *Crossing the Threshold of Hope*, Alfred A. Knopf, NY, 1994

CHAPTER NINE

Loss of Meaning

The Feeling of Meaningless-Emptiness

If symbols of one's Ultimate Concern lose their transparency to the Infinite and are not replaced with newly discovered meaningful ones, in time people will find their lives to be meaningless-empty. Nations, as well as people, may feel empty. This feeling leaves people with minimal standards for their lives; they often feel adrift and without direction. Some members of society drift into hedonism, including crime, drugs, and sexual activity without relating to the other person, which in turn intensifies the feeling of emptiness. The ultimate terror for life is meaningless-emptiness.

Several responses historically have been used when previously meaningful symbols (including concepts) have lost their meaning. They are not mutually exclusive. Several may occur simultaneously within a society, a church, or even an individual. The five types of responses Paul Tillich describes are toleration, holding on, substitution, going back, and searching for new symbols.

1. Toleration

Whether from inertia or not knowing how to proceed beyond their hopes and prayers, some churches/societies may simply tolerate the feeling of meaning-less-emptiness. They may have no other strategy.[1]

In addition to hoping and praying, to effect change these people need to dig deeper within themselves, or to seek advice from external sources to find alternatives. They need to ask questions, lots of questions, of anyone who might have even potential answers. If people don't ask the obvious questions, the whole area becomes a wasteland. When religious symbols lose their substance slowly, a wasteland develops slowly. Emptiness may drive the human mind toward strong reactions such as fanaticism or evil.[2]

Some people or societies may simply tolerate the meaningless-emptiness because they do not know how to proceed. Other people or their leaders may try to adapt by employing one or more of the other responses. If another response is found unsatisfactory, the feeling of meaningless-emptiness will return—if, indeed, it ever left.

2. Holding On

Some persist in clinging to outmoded symbols that no longer speak to the public. There is a strong tendency for clergy to hold on to deficient symbols. They may think: "These symbols have been meaningful. They should continue to be meaningful." This thinking may well lead the clergy to intensify the use of these symbols. The strategy is effective only if the setback is truly self-correcting in time.

Holding on to outmoded symbols differs from toleration in that holding on can be employed as a strategy. If the situation is truly temporary and is self-correcting, the strategy will likely be effective. People might even increase the frequency of their customary rituals and other activities.

Martin Luther posted his 95 theses on the door of the Wittenberg Palace in 1517. Despite people flocking to the new religion of Protestantism, the Roman Catholic Church's strategy was to "hold on." The Catholic Church didn't begin to reform itself until 1545. This is known as Vatican 1 in Catholic circles and as the Counter Reformation in Protestant circles.

3. Substitution

Some replace symbols representing the Infinite with finite symbols. Then no Ultimate Concern is associated with a particular symbol, group, usage, or world-view.[3] Called secularization, this response becomes more and more materialistic.

Sometimes the substituted finite symbol is abstract, such as church doctrine (as in the Inquisition), motherhood, materialism, nationalism (e.g.: The Third Reich), or a particular form of government (e.g.: communism). Tillich calls the worship of anything finite "idolatry." Leaders may become adamant, oppressive, and tyrannical.

Faith is expressed in symbolic language because only symbolic language can express the Infinite.[4] Where a myth or symbols are taken as an expression of Ultimate Concern, they become part of the foundation of a religious community. As such, they cannot be replaced by philosophy or by an independent code of morals.[5]

If doctrines or concepts, however passionately expressed, are made absolute, they become idols rather than faith because they are without love.[6] History demonstrates terrible crimes committed in the name of doctrines, e.g.: the Inquisition. If political pressure for conformity is successful, faith has been transformed into a mere set of behavior patterns which lack love and intimacy.[7]

4. Going Back

Some try to go back to the "better" symbols and concepts of yesteryear. This strategy of returning to what worked in the past is often called *orthodoxy* or *fundamentalism*. Karen Armstrong writes that fundamentalism—whether Jewish, Christian, or Muslim—rarely arises as a battle with an external enemy. Instead it usually begins as an internal struggle in which traditionalists fight their own members whom they believe are making too many concessions to secular culture.[8]

Efforts to return to religious beliefs and practices of the past usually result in a narrowing of religious doctrine. It may be a modest movement, or it may extend to all aspects of daily living. Fundamentalism has occurred in various religions: Christianity, Hinduism, Sikhism, Buddhism, Confucianism, and both Sunni and Shiite Islam.

In *Battle for God*, Karen Armstrong says the overarching reason for moving toward fundamentalism is fear of loss of religion. Fundamentalists are fighting for survival of their faith in a world that they perceive as hostile to their religion.[9] Beginning with the Renaissance, causes of this fear have included two changes. One is a change in the world economy: people no longer entirely dependent on agriculture rely less on religious practices long intended to help ensure a good harvest needed for survival.[10] The other change is the void created as reason (Logos) displaces mythos. It is mythos that provides meaning to humans' existential issues.[11] Without mythos, logical and rational world cannot assuage grief, especially over the death of a loved one or anything as gross as the Holocaust and World War II.[12]

The move to fundamentalism often occurs after some social injustice between nations or between the haves and the have-nots, e.g.: the perceived injustice of the draft during the Vietnam War and the increase in participation in the conservative churches. Islamic fundamentalism was a weak and insignificant movement until the partitioning of Palestine, the taking of Palestinian lands without compensation, and the defeats of the Arab nations in the 1967 war. They suffered great uncertainty over extended periods of time: "Where will we live?" "Will we ever be able to return to our homes?" Perhaps most importantly, "Why did Allah turn his back to us?" When these thoughts and feelings are held over an extended period of time, they create fertile soil for fundamentalism.[13]

After the 9/11 destruction of the World Trade Center and the attack on the Pentagon, several prominent evangelists proclaimed that the tragedy had been a punishment from God for secularism in the United States.[14] Religious leaders who believe the current difficulties of their society are caused by trivializing religion are apt to make the religion more literal, rigid, and narrow in its doctrine. They strive to make the religion less tolerant of deviation.

Three broad groups of fundamentalists are distinguished based on their view of the outside world. The *mild fundamentalists* include the Protestant Reformation of the 16th century, which broke from Catholicism. This group also includes the Evangelical religions in the United States today. The Bahais, which were founded in Persia (Iran) in the 19th century, declared they were returning to the truer and fundamental principles of Islam. They stress the tenets and doctrines of an earlier time and a more rigorous (perhaps more literal) interpretation of their texts.

The second group is *modern fundamentalists*, who tend to isolate their followers from the mainstream of secular life. They include the Essenes of Biblical Times and many cults of the 20th century, including David Koresh and his Branch Davidians. This group also includes the early years of the People's Temple, before Jim Jones and his followers got into drugs and developed paranoid obsessions.

The third group is the *radical extremists*, who feel that everyone who is not with them is either against them or is irrelevant. They are willing to use force and violence to impose their own values on their society and others. With this goal in mind, they are engaged in politics, or even terrorism or war. They include suicide bombers and other terrorists, and the Ku Klux Klan when they were lynching, burning, and bombing to block racial integration in the United States from the end of the Civil War through the 1960s.

Fundamentalists usually adopt some written document as their unquestionable authority, such as the *Bible* or the *Qur'an*. They hold their document to be not only from God, but literal, free of errors in transmission and in their leaders' application of its principles. The more radical fundamentalists tend to have a low tolerance for ambiguity. They want answers. They believe God communicates with their leader(s), and the leaders relay these communications to the people. The communications must be obeyed. Their organization is typically authoritarian. At times some of these religious authorities resort to coercion and force, thus becoming demagogues and tyrants.

Radical extremists need enemies. They tend to select one aspect of the culture to despise, then use it to symbolize all the evils in the culture. They divide the world and people into those that are good and those that are evil. Their followers may consider themselves an elite cadre. They may extend their religious beliefs to every aspect of their lives. They are prideful, as many considered the

Pharisees. They often differentiate themselves from the rest of a population by their dress and by living in enclaves, thereby reducing exposure to the "outside" world. They are often evangelistic: "If I know the Truth and you don't, it is my responsibility to enlighten you." Christian fundamentalists draw heavily from the biblical books of Daniel and Revelation. "The end" is often pictured as being ushered in by a savior: The Messiah in the Jewish faith, Christ in the Christian faith, and the hidden Imam of Islam.[15]

The egocentricity of the leader can generate belief that the group, and with it the whole world, will also end violently. This belief, combined with their need for enemies and their desire to impose their beliefs on the rest of society, can lead the cult to arming itself. The fire is fanned by their beliefs in afterlife rewards for their martyrdom and righteousness.

David Koresh of the Branch Davidians of Waco, Texas, anticipated the world ending in conflagration. This group split from the Seventh Day Adventists. The Branch Davidians thought David Koresh was the last prophet. They believed in the imminent return of Jesus Christ. Koresh said the apocalypse of the end of the world would begin when the U.S. Army attacked, so they armed their compound. Bureau of Alcohol, Tobacco, Firearms and Explosives (ATF) agents obtained a search warrant alleging violations of gun laws and the possibility of explosives. When the ATF agents tried to serve the warrant, the Branch Davidians killed four agents. Six Branch Davidians also were killed. After a 51-day standoff, the U.S. authorities brought in tanks. A massive fire erupted in the compound. An investigation concluded that the fires were started by the Branch Davidians. Seventy-six followers of Koresh died, including more than twenty children.

Fundamentalism is to religion as fascism is to government. Both are authoritarian, and want to control details of daily life. Neither allows dissent or open discussion. Each may restrict gatherings that are not controlled by their authorities.

If myths are interpreted literally, philosophy must reject them as absurd, and if the religion takes its myths of faith literally, they become idolatrous. Literalism deprives God of his timeliness and of his majesty.[16] The symbols of faith do not appear in isolation. They are incorporated in stories of encounters between human(s) and "the god(s)." There is no substitute for the use of symbols in myths. Myths are the language of faith.[17] Other than discovering a new symbol that does reflect the Ultimate, in time all of the above alternatives will prove unsatisfactory, resulting in the people and their nation finding their lives empty.

5. Searching for New Symbols

As symbols lose their meaning, many people search for new symbols that also represent the Infinite. However, only symbolic language can express the Infinite. New symbols cannot be created, but they can be reinterpreted.[18] They can only be discovered in the sense of being recognized. "I'm not sure exactly what I'm looking for, but I expect to know it when I find it."

When old symbols have lost their transparency to the Infinite and no new symbols are available yet, the search itself may become a "stand-in" symbol that acknowledges the absence of a meaningful transcendent symbol. This has come to be known figuratively as "the search for the Holy Grail." Everyone must enter the forest (the unknown) by his or her own path. In other words, each individual needs to conduct his or her own search. In America today, many seem to be living in this situation, yet few are able to succeed alone. The result for many people has been the shift from organized religion per se to a search for more personal, individualized spirituality.

On one hand, the feeling of emptiness, of being "lost" or without orientation, is the dissonance between the feeling of reverence and the idealized way to live. On the other hand, it is the loss of compatible beliefs and other thought concepts. In an effort to hold on to the feelings and actions, some people psychologically move from religion, with its doctrines of belief, to spirituality.

The awareness of transcendence remains very active in Americans' hearts and minds. This awareness seems to be ubiquitous in all humans. Huston Smith pointed out that every society had believed in deities or other supernatural agents until the 20th century. Communistic USSR and China were the exceptions. Many Americans say they are spiritual but not religious. They recognize within themselves the ubiquitous human need to relate to something greater than the self—to the Ultimate. They are searching for "contact" with some manifestation of transcendent power.

Robert Wuthnow, a religious sociologist, in his book *After Heaven, Spirituality in America Since 1950*, described this shift in focus of American religious faith and spirituality from sacred places (church and synagogue) to an urge or drive to search for contact with the transcendent spirituality.

The search can take many forms. It is characteristic that each searcher gets input from multiple and diverse sources, yet each person feels alone, even in a congregation with fellow seekers, and as with the search for the Holy Grail, the search itself can become more important than its goal.

Religious Coercion

Whether religious authorities attempt to hold on to doctrines or substitute finite concepts, presenting them as objects to be venerated, or whether they advocate a return to the prior religious symbols of earlier days, there are two potential complications. One is idolatry. The other is the use of force or coercion to obtain compliance. In the process, religious authorities may become tyrannical. The Inquisition is an example. If there is no official hierarchy, the feeling of meaningless-emptiness may amount to a call for a charismatic leader(s) who advocates one of the other alternatives.

Idolatry is defined as elevating something finite to the status of Infinite. The opposite of mysticism, therefore, is not rationalism, but rather whatever theology is demanded by religious authority. Historically, it has been the poets, mystics, and prophets who have proclaimed the idolatry of misguidedly worshiping something finite for itself alone. Whenever religion becomes fanatical, love is diverted from other people to the championed cause, e.g.: communism.[19] Not only will the feeling of meaningless-emptiness grow, but the elevated finite object or idea may damage or destroy other finite objects or ideas.

The ability to coerce reduces the dependence on sanctity or meaningful symbols, and replaces it with religious authority. As ecclesiastical power increases, the relationship between sanctity and authority is likely to become inverted, with authority dominating.[20] Written codification may over-sanctify the specific, making the expression of moral principles characteristic of particular times and places, supplanting and trivializing the general principals themselves.[21] The reform movement in Judaism was an update of the sacred, moving it away from trivialization, e.g.: the prohibition against eating pork no longer signified holiness, but trivialized holiness. A large number of American Jews abandoned this taboo without abandoning their Judaism.[22] This movement, called Reform Judaism, has its own synagogues.

When acceptance is coerced, it becomes a lie. There can be no genuine or binding "yes" unless "no" is an option. The lie of coercion is the lie of the oppressor, not of the one who is coerced. Authority coercing acceptance of its doctrine distorts the foundation of its own authority—the sanctity of its rituals.[23] Rituals become part of the deceit if they lead the faithful into bondage while promising salvation.[24] The sacred and the numinous may become detached from each other and from their corrective functions. The act of ritual acceptance, once more powerful than belief, becomes a proverbial form of hypocrisy. Rituals become empty and meaningless. Within an individual there may be alienation from the deeper parts of the self.[25] Humans require meaningfulness. In a society devoid of intrinsic meaning, humans must fabricate meaning.[26]

If the leadership of a religious organization is hierarchical, and if the hierarchy feels threatened, it may attempt to substitute its doctrine and its symbols for objects of veneration instead of using them to point to the Ultimate. Tillich labels this idolatry.[27] He gives the example of deifying motherhood, which will impact children and is apt to prevent a son from having a fulfilling relationship with a woman.[28]

Religious authorities may interpret "the current terrible situation," and lack of response to the prayers for divine help, as some failing on the part of society. They might believe that the people have "sinned" or have not made adequate sacrifices, or that the rituals of worship or supplication were not performed sincerely and accurately. In the Judeo-Christian traditions, there are precedents for such interpretations. God destroyed the world by flood (except for Noah and his relatives) because of the people's sins. God also destroyed the cities of Sodom and Gomorrah for the same reason. The prophets Isaiah, Jeremiah, Amos, and Hosea foretold the wrath of God against his people unless they repented. These prophesies were actualized by the Babylon captivity and the destruction of the Jewish temple in Jerusalem.

Even the pagans held such views: Jupiter was the chief and the most powerful god of the Romans. He was the god who hurled thunderbolts. As such, he was the Guardian of the City of Rome. He was the god who guided the Roman Republic to its greatness, to control over "all the world." His magnificent temple in the Roman capital was covered with gold. In 83 BCE, lightning destroyed the temple, and the resulting fire destroyed much of the city. Why? Because Jupiter was angry with the people of Rome! That was the only feasible reason. But why?

> Jupiter used to be with us. Now we must have displeased him. Even though we don't understand how or why, let us return to "the good old days" when life was comfortable, predictable, and secure—when god was in his temple and all was right with the world.[29]

Huston Smith's Search

Huston Smith's search for religious understanding extended over most of his adult life. He immersed himself in different world religions for years at a time in order to experience each religion and its spirituality as an adherent from the inside. Finally, he returned to the religion of his boyhood as a Methodist Christian. He stated:

> If we take the world's enduring religions at their best, we discover the distilled wisdom of the human race.[30]

Kim Kerfott's Search

Kim Kerfott spoke in the candle-lighting ritual of the Unitarian Universalist Church she had just joined. Held in January 1999, that service was one of the first in a spacious new building.

> I am no stranger to moving. I have had 41 mailing addresses in 43 years. I have also moved around a lot spiritually.

> My mother tried to raise me Mormon, but it didn't work, probably because I take after my grandfather. He lost his professorship at Brigham Young University for teaching evolution in a religion course. He went astray, but I have wandered from the beginning.

> I chanted with Buddhists in Brooklyn. I was banished by the Boston Moonies for asking too many questions. So much for free food and living quarters. I retreated with Maritime Jesuits who shared their homemade wine and throaty folksongs. I studied transcendental meditation, Texas-style. I dated members of Jerry Falwell's church while preaching at the Church of the Covenant. I was simultaneously comforted and terrified in, of all places, Toledo, Ohio, by the goddess Sekhemt.

> I participated in Lakota sweat lodges in the East, South, West, and North, and was twice honored to be at Sun Dances in Medicine Wheel. I experienced Catholic mass in Spanish at sunrise on the Island of Margarita, led by priests who went to prison for teaching adults to read.

> I danced in women's circles and African drum circles all over the place, which is, incidentally, descriptive of how I dance. I witnessed for the Druid Hills Baptist Church, but that doesn't count since I was just trying to get the power minister to give me his dog, which, I note, was never born again. To this day I don't understand what the

Atlanta Existentialist Congregation believed, but I did learn not to let that bother me.

Over one twelve-month period I visited more than fifty different churches, but I never joined a single one. That is, until last week, when I joined this church. For me, joining is about finding a home, but it is not about settling down. Joining is about committing to move, not alone, but with company. It is about deciding to participate with a special family in spiritual exploration and social actions. It is a promise to embrace fellow travelers as we all move forward, backward, up, down, in circles, or just jiggle in place. It is an affirmation that I will continue to undertake both independent and collective practical action to improve our local and world communities.

Unitarian Universalism seems to me to be a luxury mobile home for the soul shared by a paisley-colored gypsy band which is hell-bent on trying to bring positive change to the transient planet, our lovely earth, which is endlessly rotating while hurling through space.

I am energized with outward activity and inward motion, and I am thoroughly convinced that there is inspiration for both here. It was gently reassuring to me to witness the spirit generated by this group in its relocation. The move made me feel stable and at home. Thank you for that. Also, thank you for this big, beautiful space!

So, I light the candle with the hope that everyone will feel as welcomed and comfortable as I do in this new place. May everyone be blessed to experience the exhilaration of motion, and the joy of thoughtful change!

—Kim Kerfott, January 31, 1999

The Search is Lonely

The need to search alone is not motivated by a lack of intimacy or unwillingness to be vulnerable. Rather, the aloneness arises from the need to examine one's own life in relation to the Ultimate. This need is as old as Socrates: "The unexamined life is not worth living." This principle was reiterated in the story of those searching for the Grail.

Wuthnow pointed out that Thomas Jefferson gave two reasons for the free exercise of religion; they are valid today. First, the human spirit is naturally inclined to think freely, to be curious, to examine alternatives, and to be influenced by arguments that seem reasonable. Second, any conviction arrived at short of free exploration is likely to be less than genuine.[31] No one can tell another when he/she has found his goal or that he/she has searched enough.

NOTES FOR CHAPTER NINE

9.1   Brown, D. MacKenzie: *Ultimate Concern, Tillich in Dialogues*, Harper and Row, New York City, 1965, p. 34

9.2   Brown: p. 180-1

9.3   Brown: p. 25 & 38

9.4   Tillich, Paul: *Dynamics of Faith*, Harper Torah Books, NYC, 1957, p. 44

9.5   Tillich, Paul: *A History of Christian Thought*, Touchstone Books, Simon & Schuster, NY, 1967, p. 121

9.6   Tillich: p. 113

9.7   Tillich: p. 27

9.8   Armstrong, Karen: *The Battle for God*, Ballantine Publishing Group, New York, 2000, p. 110

9.9   Armstrong: p. vii

9.10 Armstrong: p. xv

9.11 Armstrong: p. 182

9.12 Armstrong: p. 13 & 365

9.13 Armstrong: p. 352

9.14 Armstrong: p. viii

9.15 Phifer, Kenneth: Sermons Feb 4 & 11, 2002

9.16 Tillich: p. 52

9.17 Tillich: p. 48-51

9.18 Brown: p. 89

9.19 Brown: p. 60

9.20 Rappaport: p. 446

9.21 Rappaport: p. 445

9.22 Rappaport: p. 445

9.23 Rappaport: p. 446

9.24 Rappaport: p. 447

9.25 Rappaport: p. 447-8

9.26 Rappaport: p. 451

9.27 Brown: *Ultimate Concern*, p. 29, and Tillich, Paul: *A History of Christian Thought*, Touchstone Books, Simon & Schuster, NY, 1967, p.318

9.28 Brown: p. 24

9.29 Holland, Tom, cited: *Rubicon, The Last Years of the Roman Republic*, Doubleday, NYC, 2003, p. 82-85

9.30 Moyer, Bill: *The Wisdom of Faith*, Public Affairs Television Inc. Interview with Huston Smith, Newbridge Communications Inc., 1996

9.31 Wuthnow, Robert: *After Heaven, Spirituality in America Since 1950*, University of California Press, Berkley & Los Angeles, 1998, p. 58

CHAPTER TEN

Religious Beliefs Can Be Troublesome

Confabulation

The human mind is inquisitive; it also synthesizes and integrates. The mind constructs and constantly updates a mental model of the world. The mind ponders important intellectual questions, meditates on them, "works" on them during sleep, and dreams of them. The more critical the issue, the more determined the human mind is to arrive at an answer(s), even when there seems to be none. The mind tends to fill important gaps with the best, the most meaningful facts or concepts available. This process is called *confabulation*.

Confabulation is not meant to deceive the self or others. Religious seers and leaders have sincere confidence that "*this* is the way it must be." Initially, they are usually aware that they "filled in the gap." In time, that distinction may be ignored or even forgotten. Certainly, by the time the concept(s) pass to successive generations, the distinction has lost any significance.

Bases of Confabulation

In religion, any confabulated theory is often based on some combination of the following:

- **The society's views of cosmology.** For example, the Aztecs believed that gods sacrificed themselves to create the sun, and that daily human blood sacrifices were necessary to assist the gods to make the sun rise each day.[1]

- **The current political situations of the society.** These include both internal and external situations. For example, Roman Emperor Constantine used Christianity to meet the need for a unifying force for the empire.

- **The subsistence resources of the society.** For example, some primitive societies made a deity of the animal that was their chief source of food.

- **The critical resources that are in short supply.** For example, rain gods are found only in semi-arid environments. They are not found in rainforests or in deserts.

- **The society's prior religious systems of belief.** For example, Moses built on Abraham; Christianity built on the prophesy of the coming Messiah in Judaism; Mohammad included parts of Judaism and of Christianity in Islam.

- **The story of a society's founder.** This may include any or all of the founder's life history. For example, in *The Birth of the Messiah*, Raymond Browne describes how theological meanings in the life of Jesus began with his crucifixion and were developed in reverse chronological order.[2]

These are exemplified in Denise and John Carmody's description of how the mystic uses his own background and that of his culture to cast the description of his mystical experience.[3] Young children also use confabulation; Jean Piaget asked his child, "What makes the wind blow?" The child answered, "Because the wind wants to get from one place to another." Piaget's child anthropomorphized the wind. Karen Armstrong said, "All religions must begin with some anthropomorphism."[4]

"A deity which is utterly remote from humanity, such as Aristotle's Unmoved Mover, cannot inspire a spiritual quest."[5] The god in Genesis walked in the garden with Adam and Eve. He wrestled with Jacob. Later this god became a symbol of transcendence. The deities of Greece were in human form with human emotions and foibles. Greek gods represented the intrinsic forces of nature and of humans: thunder and lightning, the sun moving across the heavens, the sea, sexual attraction, the institution of the home, etc. The biggest distinction between gods and humans in ancient Greece was that the gods had what Greeks and many other humans craved: immortality. The Hebrews did not "lust" after immortality. Immortality of gods may be the best—but is not the only way—to pass a religion across generations.

Assumptions About Religious Messages

Religious messages gain much of their power from the perception that they speak only truth. In *In God We Trust*, Scott Atran explains:

> That one significant distinction between fantasy and religion is knowledge of its source. People know or assume that public fictions (novels, movies, cartoons, etc.) were created by specific people who had particular intentions for doing so. Religious believers, however, tend to assume that the utterances or texts connected with religious doctrines are authorless, timeless, and true. Consequently, they often

don't apply ordinary relevance criteria to religious communications to figure out the speaker's true intentions or check on whether God is lying or lacking information. Timelessness implies that cues from the surrounding environment, background knowledge, and memory are all irrelevant. So God's message can apply to any context and to each context indefinitely many and different ways.[6]

What the religious leaders of successive generations do recognize is their own vested interest in current beliefs and practices. They also realize, and many point out, that any religion in its current form has met the critical needs of society for some time. No one likes change. No one likes uncertainty. No one likes to lose power and influence.

Violence and Religion

The frequency and ferocity of raids by Mongolians were so severe that China built a wall. Similarly, the raids of the Norsemen (Vikings) on England and other European countries gave rise to several lines of *The Book of Common Prayer*. "From the wrath of the Norsemen, good God protect us."

When religious leaders perceive they or their religion is under attack, they move to define themselves more clearly. Every definition involves exclusions. Tillich believes that this self-definition inevitably results in a narrowing down and becoming less tolerant of other religions.[7] People have been burned at the stake, and religious wars have been fought over systems of belief and their symbols. Religious wars are not fought solely over feelings of awe and reverence, nor over acts of compassion. Schleiermacher said morals are the same in all religions.[8] Further, all religions admonish their followers to love others, to express compassion, to stand for social justice, and to forgive others and seek forgiveness. Schleiermacher said that religion is feeling, and that religion cannot and will never originate in pure knowledge (from only thoughts.)[9]

Before monotheism, wars did not originate over religious issues. The newer god was simply added to the community of worshiped gods, or an established god assumed an additional name and, perhaps, attributes.[10] In other words, too many societies with monotheistic religions have held that: *If your confabulation is significantly different from mine, that is adequate reason to go to war and try to kill each other.*

Why Violence? The question is, Why have religion and violence, including war, been so tied together? This is particularly puzzling since the core feeling of the Infinite is so similar in all religions. So, why is there such intolerance among the religions? What accounts for all the religious animosity between or among religions? Surely it cannot reasonably be attributed solely to differences in beliefs, even recognizing that many may have arisen from confabulations... or can it?

People of the Axial Age put spirituality, compassion, and The Golden Rule at the apex of their goals. They also stressed what people were to avoid: selfishness at the expense of another, greed, egotism, hatred, and violence. These goals need to be kept in mind. If one concentrates only on the negative, one is apt to become cynical, depressed, and hopeless. If one concentrates only on what one is striving for, and becomes dogmatic about it, one is apt to develop an attitude of superiority and an inquisitorial stridency.[11] All the world's religions have seen eruptions of this type of self-righteous, militant piety.[12]

Test For Religions: Karen Armstrong said the test for a religion is simple: If people's beliefs (doctrines) lead them to be belligerent, intolerant, and unkind toward others' faith, they are on the wrong path. If, however, their convictions impel them to acts of compassion and to honor the stranger, then their beliefs are good, helpful, and sound. "This is the test of true religiosity in every single one of the major traditions." Religious doctrines usually have imbedded in them a program for action. If people behave in a Christ-like manner, they will discover or rediscover the truth about Jesus and associated beliefs.[13]

Religions Are Not Necessarily at Odds

The people of China generally are eclectic in their choices among the principles of Buddhism, Taoism, and Confucianism. They find no incompatibility in mixing these religious teachings to suit themselves. Similarly, many Japanese choose among the principles of Shintoism and Buddhism. Yet, the three monotheistic religions—Judaism, Christianity, and Islam—have experienced animosity over the centuries, interspersed with periods of tranquility. Why?

There have been wars that in the beginning seemed motivated primarily by religion, such as the domestic crusade against the Cathars. At the other end of the continuum are wars with negligible religious involvement, such as WWI and WWII. In the war for the liberation of Kuwait from Saddam Hussein and Iraq, the United Nations kept religious issues out, even when Iraq tried to move it toward a religious conflict by firing scud missiles against Israel. Had Israel counter-attacked, the supposition was that many Arab nations would have sided against Israel.

In *When Religion Becomes Evil*, Charles Kimball, a student of religion and violence, asserted that "more wars have been waged, more people killed, and more evil perpetrated in the name of religion than by any other institutional force in human history."[14] I believe the general concept of a causal relationship between religion and violence is overblown.

Religions Become Embroiled

Just because wars, killings, and acts of evil are committed in the name of religion does not mean that religion was the prime motivating force or the original cause. Paul Tillich referred to religion as a person's or a society's Ultimate Concern. Survival of any society ranks high on its list of concerns. Often the roles of the aggressive society and the defending society are so muddled that this distinction cannot be assigned. Further, both aggressors know that attacking the other's religious institutions is attacking its Ultimate Concern, and can cause demoralization and disorientation among the people.

Religions also become embroiled in conflicts of other origins because the people seek divine help to prevail over their enemies and to bolster public support for the war. Hence, they try to create as many reasons for the armed conflict as possible. If people don't support the war on one basis, they may do so for one of the other reasons. Differences in religions may be stressed to psychologically separate *them* from *us*, and to demean the foe to a sub-human status.

When humans treat others or groups of others without respect or love, but rather with demeaning attitudes and behavior, the principles of cognitive dissonance and mental harmony cause them to regard the others as grossly inferior and not deserving of decency, e.g.: the behavior of whites toward Native Americans and African slaves.

Destroying Temples Equals Destroying Opponents

In ancient times, one side commonly attacked the other's religious institutions, destroying the other's temples. Roman authorities would transport the statues of the gods of a conquered people to Rome as symbols of conquest. The conquered people who were brought to Rome had their gods there, also, for it was generally believed that the god had to follow the statue. Some people actually believed that the statue was the god. In Rome and other polytheistic societies, the imported god was simply added to the Pantheon of gods. If the function of the god had a counterpart among the Roman gods, then the Roman god was simply given an additional duty or an additional name. The conquered people who were left in their homeland had lost their temples and statues, as well as their sense of divine help and protection, even in their daily tasks. They were left without objects of devotion, without a sense of their place in the world, and without supernatural support.

Hebrew Religion Is an Exception

The Hebrews were not dependent on any finite object. For the times, it was a stroke of genius that the Ten Commandments contained a prohibition of having statues of God: "You shall not make for yourself an idol in the form of anything in heaven above or on the earth beneath or in the waters below."[15] Even after the Ark of the Covenant was captured, the Israelites continued their faith. Similarly, when the temple was destroyed by the Babylonians in 587 BCE, and the second temple was destroyed by the Romans in 70 CE, the Israelites maintained their faith. Jeremiah realized that the Jewish faith was not dependent on materialistic symbols—nothing finite. God says, I will put my law within them and I will write it upon their hearts…even on the strict interpretation of the law.[16] Walter Brueggemann comments on this passage as a new covenant between God and his people. "The Torah that marks the new community is not a practice of law to clobber people, not a censure to expel and scold people, not a picky legalism. It is rather a release from small moralisms to see things through the eyes of God's passion and anguish. The Torah is a reminder that God's will focuses on large human questions and that we also may focus on weighty matters of justice, mercy, and righteousness."[17]

Most Catholic churches have included statues of Jesus (God) in their churches and cathedrals. The Protestants have observed this commandment more strictly. After the reformation, the fear of committing idolatry resulted in Protestants destroying many beautiful artifacts in previously Catholic churches, artifacts that today would be very precious and valuable.[18] The Sunni Muslims took this commandment even more seriously. Since humans were made in God's image, any image of a human was considered a violation of this commandment. As a result, there are very few portraits or statues of humans or Allah in the Muslim world, although the Shiite Muslims do have pictures of Ali, the son-in-law of Mohammad. The creative artistic spirit of Muslims found a major outlet in geometric designs.

In Hinduism there has been a concern that images must be used carefully, lest they engender the belief that the image is adequate to describe the Ultimate Mystery. Hinduism has tried to mediate divine reality without slipping into idolatry. The many concepts and statues of the Divine are considered different expressions of the one Ultimate Reality, Brahman. Brahman is unknown and unknowable. The very number of gods and their complex manifestations in many ways is so outrageous and so overwhelming that it reminds us of the unspeakable nature of divine reality. Images of the Divine may or may not be anthropomorphic. Those that are not include natural phenomena such as stones, earthen mounds, trees, rivers, and celestial bodies. The unrealistic images are to be a constant reminder that Brahman is not like humans.[19]

Refusal to Worship Society's Gods Is Treason

In ancient societies gods were commonly considered territorial. Societies frequently took failure to worship their gods as treason. The failure might be taken by the god as a slight or even as hostility. It was feared that the god might retaliate. The Old Testament specifies the killing of any member of society who worshiped "other gods." Durant stated that Jesus accepted this tradition based on John 15:6:

> If anyone abide not in me, he shall be cast forth as a branch, and shall wither; and they shall gather him up, and cast him into the fire, and he burneth.[20]

Socrates of Athens was charged with refusing to worship the gods of Athens, and thereby corrupting youth. He was sentenced to death by drinking hemlock.

When the Roman Empire fell apart, the power vacuum was filled by the Roman Catholic Church. The Church had the organization, the inclination, the finances, and the authority. It had the final word on what was right and acceptable to God. This power was undisputed during the feudal period for close to a thousand years.

It is explicitly stated in both Islam and Hinduism that an attack on the religion is not to be tolerated, which is evidence that religion was (is) their Ultimate Concern.

When new insights and new religious ideas are put forward, the established religious authorities often feel both indignant and threatened. Very few take kindly to their power and prerogatives being threatened or curtailed. With feelings of superiority and self-righteousness, they may strike out with ethnic cleansing, enslavement, inquisitions, charges of heresy with death sentences, or even armed invasions.

The Crusades

Some people believe that the Crusades to capture Jerusalem were motivated purely by religious issues, but other issues were intertwined. The invention of the horse collar circa 900 CE allowed the horse to pull a plow against his shoulders rather than against his wind pipe. This allowed the horse to do five times the work in the same amount of time. As a result, food production rose. There were fewer deaths, especially of infants. A population explosion resulted in Northern Europe.[21] Within two centuries, the land of family farms had been divided for inheritance by the sons so many times that the size of the farms was no longer adequate to support each family. By the 11th century, Europe was so prosperous that a number of people took pilgrimages to Jerusalem and other places. The Seljuk Turks, who held the Holy Land, were molesting the pilgrims. Also, the Seljuk Turks were threatening the Byzantine Empire with its seat at Constantinople, and the emperor there asked the Pope for help. All of these intertwining forces were incorporated in the speech by Pope Urban II in 1095 that proposed the Crusades to the Holy Land. The Pope said that the commandment not to kill did not apply to Muslims. The benefits he stressed were adventure, loot from the wealthy Holy Land, and the fulfillment of service obligations to the king. Further, he promised forgiveness of sins, and that the soul of anyone who was killed in battle would go straight to heaven for doing God's will. This speech has been called the greatest motivational speech in the Western world. In 1099 the first crusade did capture the Holy Land, which was held until 1187.[22]

Heresies

Ideas flowed with the movement of armies and the trade that followed. By the middle of the 12th century, ideas from the East resulted in a spectacular increase in diverse religious beliefs in Europe. Many of these were held to be heresies by the Catholic Church. A *heresy* is defined as a theological opinion or doctrine that is in opposition to the orthodox doctrines of the Catholic Church. A *heretic* is a person who had believed in church doctrine, but currently believes in a heresy. As mentioned earlier, language makes the consideration of alternatives possible. The Church feared others would also change their ideas and allegiance. For this reason, heretics were considered more dangerous than infidels, who have never joined the Church.

Many clergy did not live up to their published standards of morality and social justice. They appeared corrupt and hypocritical. This laxity not only deprived the public of an adequate model for adherence to the Church's principles, but also provided openings for heresies. Bishops were selling indulgences, holy oil, and relics. Many minor heresies were protests against the secularization of the Church.[23] By 1200, there were two major groups of heretics that Pope

Innocent III felt a strong need to address. One was the Cathars. The other was the Waldensians, or "the poor men of Lyons."

The Cathars believed in two deities, one spiritual and all good, the other materialistic and evil. This concept was similar to the doctrine of Zoroastrianism of ancient Persia. This dualism is one way of "solving" the problem of an all-loving and all-powerful god allowing evil against his people. The Cathars believed in poverty, downplaying all forms of materialism. The very devout Cathars were called "perfecti," which meant they would not kill any living thing. They ate no meat, eggs, cheese, or milk, and they would abstain from sexual relationships. They criticized the Church for not adequately stressing celibacy of the clergy, and for not stressing spirituality. In pairs, they traveled throughout Europe, spreading their ideas. In France the Cathars were also known as Albigensians for the area in which they were concentrated. The Church feared the Cathars' criticism of the Church's materialism, wealth, and worldly power.[24]

The Waldensians felt the Church had become corrupt since its founding. They desired to return to the preaching modeled on the life of Jesus. They rejected the authority of the priesthood, infant baptism, veneration of saints and martyrs, and the need for large edifices in which to worship. This was a move toward fundamentalism.

Before the Inquisition was fully organized, the Church authorized a crusade against the Cathars who inhabited the Albigensia area in Southern France. The Church offered the same indulgences for this crusade as it had for crusades to the Holy Land: forgiveness of past sins, and the martyr's palm in case of death in the field. In addition to loot, the Pope offered the lands of the Cathars to any Christians who could seize them. For many, the inducements were more powerful than strictly religious motives. One knight who had been commanded by the papal legate to expel the Cathars from their lands asked, "How can we do it? We have been brought up with these people, we have kindred among them, and we see them living righteously." The Church responded by recruiting knights and others from Germany and Italy to fight the Cathars. They breached the castle wall of the Cathars in 1209, and slew 20,000 men, women, and children.[25]

As can be seen from the definition of heresy and from the knight's question, the primary issue was neither religious feelings nor religious actions for the people to live by, but rather issues of doctrine—that is, of thought. Of course, other issues became intertwined: economics and religious authority.

Purpose of Inquisition

The Roman Catholic Church did launch the Court of Inquisition. The purpose and scope of one inquisition are best expressed by a bull of Pope Nicholas III in 1280:

> We hereby excommunicate and anathematize all heretics—Cathari, Patarines, Poor Men of Lyons…and all others, by whatever name they may be called. When condemned by the Church they shall be given over to the secular judge to be punished… If any, after being seized, repent and wish to do penance, they shall be imprisoned for life…. All who receive, defend, or aid heretics shall be excommunicated. If anyone remains under excommunication a year and a day, he shall be proscribed…If those who are suspected of heresy cannot prove their innocence, they shall be excommunicated. If they remain under the ban of excommunication a year, they shall be condemned as heretics. They shall have no right of appeal….We prohibit all laymen to discuss matters of the Catholic faith; if anyone does so he shall be excommunicated. Whoever knows of heretics, or of those who hold secret meetings, or of those who do not conform in all respects to the orthodox faith, shall make it known to his confessor, or to someone else who will bring it to the knowledge of the bishop or the inquisitor. If he does not do so he shall be excommunicated. Heretics and all who receive, support, or aid them, and all their children to the second generation, shall not be admitted to an ecclesiastical office….We now deprive all such of the benefices forever.[26]

Throughout the inquisitions, the Church maintained that it never executed anyone; rather those who had been pronounced guilty were turned over to the secular authorities for burning at the stake or other punishment. (St. John, cited earlier, and *Bible*, Matthew 7:15-20 were the scriptural reference for the burning of heretics.) The states with some reluctance nevertheless joined in prosecuting heretics because they feared that it would be impossible to govern without the aid of the Church.[27] Heretics were required to inform on other possible heretics under threat of torture. Torture was allowed to elicit confessions. A person could have his torture suspended, then be placed in prison for an indefinite time until questioning and torture were restarted. A heretic's home was often destroyed and forbidden to be rebuilt. A heretic's property could be confiscated, and usually was. In some jurisdictions part of the proceeds from property forfeitures went to the interrogators. If a person was judged a heretic after his death, his body would be exhumed, his bones burned, and the property he left his heirs confiscated. The children of heretics would be deprived of certain rights through the second generation. To make an accusation of heresy against another was a sure way to destroy one's enemies.[28]

Inquisitions Exemplify Self-perpetuation

Through the years, the inquisitions went through a number of changes, adapting to focus on new targets as interest in—or the prevalence of—previous heresies faded. This action illustrates how a large and well-organized institution such as the Court of Inquisition will always come up with a new task to perpetuate itself.[29] Witchcraft and sorcery were added to their list of charges, which gave serious credence to those practices in the minds of the public.[30] 200,000 to a million "witches" were condemned by the Inquisition.[31] In the 16th century, identifying books to be prohibited came next.[32] Then attention shifted to artistic painting. Freemasons were later added to the list. The last recorded execution for heresy took place in 1826.[33]

It is impossible to obtain a reliable estimate on the number of deaths attributed to the inquisitions. Both the inquisitors and the critics had a need to inflate the numbers, the inquisitors to show their superiors what a good job they were doing, and the critics to emphasize the evil nature of the institution.

The Holocaust showed that a secular ideology is also capable of disregarding the value of human life, even of its own citizens, and can be just as evil as the Church with its Court of Inquisition.

The Reformation

Absolute power corrupts, and in the 14th century a number of abuses were occurring in the Catholic Church. The Church was building St. Peter's Cathedral at the Vatican. A monk named Martin Luther felt that in the church's efforts to raise money for construction, it lost sight of some parts of its missions and of its principles. In an effort to reform the Church, Martin Luther wrote a list of 95 proposed revisions. As was the custom, in 1517 he posted them on the church door. Feeling threatened, the authorities moved to arrest Luther on charges of heresy, presumably to put him on trial and kill him, just as they had done to John Huss. Luther was protected by a feudal lord who was also an elector of the Holy Roman Empire. The Church had been collecting significant sums of money from the territories of the feudal lords. The "princes," as the feudal lords came to be called, realized they could keep those sums if they broke with the Catholic Church. Luther continued to press for his proposed reforms, but in time he realized the situation had created a full break with the Roman Catholic Church. Thus was Protestantism born. The Church adopted a strategy of "holding on" until 1545 when the Catholic Church called the Council of Trent and began to reform itself.

European Religious Wars

For 200 years there were a number of armed conflicts (wars) all over Northern Europe between those who supported the Church and Catholicism; and those who favored the princes, Protestantism, and "the nationalization" of Catholic Church property. Other issues were intertwined. One was the divine right of kings, which Martin Luther supported, versus sharing power with a legislative branch, a parliament. Of course, people on both sides had issues of personally selfish nature.

Efforts to reunite the churches of Europe encompassed a series of continuous wars from 1520 to 1659. During this period, a king or ruler of a principality would decide whether the people of his jurisdiction would be Catholic or Protestant. Then he would enforce this edict by imprisonment or death. As a result, religious sides frequently shifted for political advantage—or for life itself—rather than for religious conviction. Extended families were torn apart. The wanton rape and murder of people, and the pillage and devastation of property by gangs of guerrilla forces which no government controlled, resulted in a third of Europe's population dying from fighting, disease, or malnutrition.[34] In Germany, half the population died.[35] Many Germans and other nationals fled to other parts of the world. The American colonies were a popular destination. Many French Huguenots (Protestants) fled France for Geneva, Switzerland; and to Charleston, South Carolina. The situation was particularly bad during the phase of this extended conflict known as the Thirty Years War, 1618-1648. The reality of the devastation of these wars forced the remaining population to largely accept the principle of religious toleration.

Some Value Religious Freedom but Refuse It For Others

It is surprising that so many who struggle valiantly to obtain their religious freedom tend to deny that same freedom to others. The Puritans left England just ahead of their leader being arrested, then landed at Plymouth Rock in 1620 and founded the colony of Massachusetts. However, they in turn denied religious freedom to their own citizens. Roger Williams of Massachusetts Colony advocated complete religious freedom for all. He also believed that land should be purchased from the Indians, instead of being taken as grants from the King of England. In 1636, he learned he was about to be arrested, so he fled and, with other exiled people from Massachusetts, founded the colony of Rhode Island.

Unified Religious Beliefs Foster National Unity

Another cause of religious conflict over the centuries has been the goal of some rulers to use religion as a cohesive force for solidarity. Everyone in the society was expected to worship the same gods. Roman Emperor Constantine felt the need for a unifying force for the empire, so he called the Christian leaders together at Nicaea and forced agreement among them, which became the official Church doctrine, the Nicene Creed.

For about 600 years, Christians, Jews, and Muslims lived together relatively peacefully in the Islamic state that is now part of Spain. The marriage of Ferdinand and Isabella merged their countries, Aragon and Castile, into one, Spain. In an effort to unify the citizens of their country to one religion, Christianity, they started the Spanish Inquisition in 1483. Jews were its primary victims. In 1492, Ferdinand and Isabella captured Granada, thereby virtually eliminating organized Islam from the Iberian Peninsula. In the same year, they intensified their goal of unifying the beliefs of all their subjects.

Ferdinand and Isabella issued the Edict of Expulsion: convert to Christianity, depart, or be killed. Many Jews and Muslims converted, and many left Spain. Others went underground. The Spanish Inquisition was charged with carrying out the decree. Since anyone could be accused of not supporting the faith, there was a loss of a sense of security and well-being, and for many a constant anxiety. People's creativity and productivity suffered.[36]The kings of England, Scotland, Norway, Sweden, Denmark, Northern Germany, and Bohemia broke with Rome to nationalize their religions.

Contemporary Implications

Atrocities committed for—or at least rationalized by—religious beliefs continue in many parts of the world today. These range from individual acts of violence, to bombing large groups of innocent bystanders, to wars and genocide. Even in the United States, where the Constitution codifies a separation of religious power and political power, conflict over whether or not it is a "Christian nation" still persists. Passions over which values will infuse U.S. laws are fueled by increasing diversity in the population's beliefs. In much of the world, especially the Middle

East, entire nations still engage in deadly armed conflicts over secular-versus-religious control of institutions and daily life. These struggles often disaffect groups with less power, such as women or the region's minority religions.

Our best chances for finding common ground begin by understanding the motivations and processes of these struggles. We must study history to learn how to avoid mistakes of the past while identifying successes we can we can carry into the future. We must acknowledge that everyone has similar desires, even the least powerful among us, but sometimes we have very different approaches to pursuing them. Only then can we begin to find new ways to live in mutually beneficial harmony.

NOTES FOR CHAPTER TEN

10.1   Higgins, Kathleen: *World Philosophy*; lecture 24, The Teaching Co, Chantilly, VA

10.2   Browne, Raymond: *The Birth of the Messiah, Book II*, Anchor Bible, 1999, p. 239

10.3   Carmody, Denise & John: *Holiness East and West*, Oxford University Press, 1996, p. 12

10.4   Armstrong, Karen: *A Short History of Myth*, Conongate, New York City, 2005, p. 48

10.5   Armstrong, Karen: *A History of God*, Ballantine Books, 1994, p. 48

10.6   Atran, Scott: *In Gods We Trust*, Oxford University Press, 2002, p. 92

10.7   Tillich, Paul: *A History of Christian* Thought, Touchstone Books, Simon & Schuster, New York, 1967, p.xx; and Durant, Will: *The Story of Civilization*, Simon and Schuster, New York, p. 66

10.8   Schleiermacher, Fredrick: *On Religion*, trans. T. Tice, Knox Press, Richmond, VA, 1969, p. 304

10.9   Schleiermacher: p. 93

10.10 Durant, Will: *The Story of Civilization, Vol 3, Caesar and Christ*, Simon and Schuster, New York, 1944, p. 62

10.11 Armstrong, Karen: *The Great Transformation*, Alfred Knopf, New York City, 2006, p. 392

10.12 Armstrong: *The Great Transformation*, p. 393

10.13 Armstrong: *The Great Transformation*, p. 392

10.14 Kimball, Charles: *When Religion Becomes Evil*, HarperCollins, 2003, p. 1

10.15 *Bible*: Exodus 20:4-5

10.16 *Bible*: Jeremiah 31:31

10.17 Brueggemann, Walter: *A Social Reading of the Old Testament*, Fortress Press, Minneapolis, 1994, p. 48

10.18   Asimov, Isaac: *Asimov's Chronology of Science and Discoveries*, Harper & Row, New York City, 1989, p. 73

10.19   *Encyclopedia Britannica*, Vol 13, 15th Ed, p. 764

10.20   *Bible*: John 15:6

10.21   Burman: p. 18

10.22   Burman: p. 21

10.23   Durant: Vol 4, p. 774-5

10.24   Burman: p. 16-17

10.25   Burman: p. 18

10.26   Burman: p. 21

10.27   Burman: p. 104

10.28   Burman: p. 114

10.29   Burman: p. 179

10.30   Burman: p. 114

10.31   Burman: p. 104

10.32   Burman: p. 179

10.33   Burman: p. 100

10.34   Burman: p. 207

10.35   Armstrong, Karen: *The Battle for God*, Ballantine Publishing Group, New York, 2001, p. 6

10.36   Benton, William: *Britannica Junior Encyclopedia*, 1972, Vol. 13/RS, p. 88A

CHAPTER ELEVEN

Social Justice in Daily Life
Replaces Sacrifice

"Those who love God must love their brothers and sisters also."[1]

"Truly I tell you, just as you did it to one of the least of these who are members of my family, you did it to me"[2]

Axial Age Social Justice[3]

The immense changes of the Axial Age began with issues of social justice—action changes: not to swindle, not to disregard agreements of payment for labor, not to pay or take bribes, and to plead the case for widows and orphans. People were to be just and righteous. They were to have a conscience and no longer be playthings of the gods. Previously, various gods would take different sides in human conflicts, just as they did in the Indian legend of Mahabharata, and in the Greek and Trojan War. Nor were humans to be pawns in squabbles between or among the gods themselves, as had happened with jealousies. If humans were to be righteous and just, then God should be righteous and just, too. His interventions in human affairs were to be determined only by love for his people and justice. Further, this meant that there would be no role for other gods. Polytheism gave way to monotheism as the concepts accompanying the Axial Age spread.

Before the Axial Age, Indo-European belief in fate had spread over much of the world to varying degrees. Thus, a warrior could be more aggressive in battle, sure that whether he lived or died was a matter of fate, not the risk he took. Further, since the future was predetermined by fate, then people should be able to divine the future. This engendered soothsayers, various types of oracles, and astrologers. As the Axial Age concept of people being responsible for themselves grew, the concept of fate became passé. People were no longer to be the victims or beneficiaries of fate.

Israel and Judea

These same trends also occurred in Israel and Judea. Oracles and divinations became things of the past. Prophecy became increasingly important. Social justice and relief of suffering had been one of the purposes of Yahweh since the exodus from Egypt. Yahweh could not ignore the current cries of the oppressed: the swindling, exploitation, and lack of acts of compassion. Both Amos[4] and Jeremiah had pleaded with their people to repent. Both had prophesied disaster, which became the Babylonian destruction of their Temple and the exile of many of the people. These prophets held that the Jews had misunderstood the covenant, which meant responsibility for right attitudes and actions, not privilege. Now, first and foremost, God was to be in the actions of people toward others.

With the destruction of the Temple, Jeremiah realized that such trappings were simply symbols of a subjective mental state, which was not subject to destruction by others.

> But this is the covenant that I will make with the house of Israel after those days, says the Lord: I will put my law within them, and I will write it on their hearts; and I will be their God, and they shall be my people. No longer shall they teach one another, or say to each other, "Know the Lord," for they shall all know me, from the least of them to the greatest, says the Lord; for I will forgive their iniquity, and remember their sin no more.[5]

Again, Walter Brueggemann addressed that statement of Jeremiah 31:33 in *A Social Reading of the Old Testament*.[6] He felt that the phrase "within them" is too personalizing. He preferred, "I will put my Torah in their midst." He also felt that "I will put my law…" is misleading. He stated, "(The) Torah that marks the new community is not a practice of law to clobber people, not a censure to expel and scold people, not a picky legalism. It is rather a release from small moralisms to see things through the eyes of God's passion and anguish. The Torah is a reminder that God's will focuses on large human questions and that we also may focus on weighty matters of justice, mercy, and righteousness." The Torah turns people from self to neighbor.

God's Message in People's Hearts

Under the new covenant everyone could know God. There would be no special knowledge or privileges. Knowledge of God would mean attending to the needs of others. The community would be forgiving, just as God forgives people. With forgiveness, the past should be past. One's attitude toward another should not be with the careful management of past hurts, but rather genuine present and future hope. Forgiveness implies a genuine sharing of power.[7] It says,

"Holding a debt (perhaps a moral debt) over you is passé. I forgive you." This is the same wording used to forgive a monetary debt in current English.

Myths and life in the temple were replaced by an emphasis on daily living, life in the streets. The local synagogue became a place of study and worship, and for meeting with the community of faith. Attitudes of kindness were stressed, as well as social justice.

Judge Prophets by Their Actions

Jesus was asked how people could distinguish between false prophets and true prophets. He replied:

> Beware of false prophets, who come to you in sheep's clothing but inwardly are ravenous wolves. You will know them by their fruits. Are grapes gathered from thorns, or figs from thistles? In the same way, every good tree bears good fruit, but the bad tree bears bad fruit. A good tree cannot bear bad fruit, nor can a bad tree bear good fruit. Every tree that does not bear good fruit is cut down and thrown into the fire. Thus you will know them by their fruits .[8]

Robert Wuthnow advocated what he called practice-oriented spirituality. He stated, "Spirituality deepens only as it is practiced and the practice includes such devotional activities as prayer, meditation, contemplation, justice, and acts of service."[9] Acts of kindness, service, and social justice increase self-esteem by harmonizing one's actions with one's thoughts ("I am doing the right thing"), and by engendering feelings of love in one's neighbor as well as in oneself. When acts of service are done with others, social support is generated, stability is encouraged, the sense of fellowship is enhanced, and the community benefits. The emotions of increased self-esteem and reverence are contagious among the group members. The name(s) other group members use to refer to their Ultimate Reality, as well as their set of metaphysical beliefs, are irrelevant as long as there is mutual respect. Everyone can relate to his/her Unconditional in his/her own way.

The Divine in Every Person

The beliefs that emerged are consistent with the prescription for action—that there is a part of the Divine in everyone. Failure to respect another was failure to respect that part of God within that person. The Infinite was recognized in all things finite, including people.

Those who oppress the poor insult their Maker, but those who are kind to the needy honor him. [10]

You are gods, children of the Most High, all of you.[11]

In Hinduism the finite self is identified as *atman*. The Infinite is identified as the god *Atman*, The One Ultimate Self, or *Brahman*. Brahman lacks duality. He is not separate from the world and humans. People love the god Brahman as the parts love the whole, and in so doing they love themselves and each other. The knowledge of this coalesces with Atman in every creature. It is a mandate that rejects any difference between what is mine and what is another's. Others are to be loved more for the sake of Atman than for themselves. Because each individual is deemed a part of Atman, people accept of each other and that death is a return to the whole.[12]

Once Jesus was asked by the Pharisees when the kingdom of God was coming, and he answered, "The kingdom of God is not coming with things that can be observed; nor will they say, 'Look, here it is!' or 'There it is!' For, in fact, the kingdom of God is among you."[13]

Another Form of Idolatry

The concept that part of the Divine is in every person can be carried to the extreme of self-adoration. This excessive pride may elevate someone toward the realm of the Divine, or it may remain earthbound and generate feelings of superiority and self-righteousness. With such a feeling or attitude, the person no longer loves his neighbor as himself, but loves himself more, and comes to believe that he/she deserves "more"—more recognition, more rewards, more of the good things of life. Forgiveness of others fades. Giving of alms begins to be motivated by show. Social justice is replaced by an air of greater entitlement, even at another's expense. The divinity within is no longer transparent of the Ultimate. Self-absorption has displaced the worship of the Ultimate. This form of pride may be limited to one individual, to a family, to a sect, or to the whole religion. An outstanding example of such pride is the description of the Pharisees in the *Bible* during the time of Jesus.

The Pharisees were a sect of Judaism that emerged after the Jews returned from Babylon in 585 BCE. In the beginning they insisted on the binding force of the oral traditions as well as the Torah. When the first part of the Talmud was written, about 200 BCE, it incorporated the Pharisees' teaching on Jewish law.

However, they believed that common sense must be used in interpreting and applying the law.[14] The Pharisees firmly believed a part of God was within every Jewish man. They believed Israel was called to be a nation of priests, and that God could be present in the humblest home, as well as the Temple. All Pharisee men observed the purity laws of the priests. They were passionately spiritual. They believed they could approach God directly without a priest or elaborate ritual. They could atone for their sins by acts of loving kindness.[15] God hated any lack of harmony in the community. Humanity is sacred. An offence against others was a denial of God, who had made man in his own image. To humiliate anyone, even a goy or a slave, was a serious offence, because it was equivalent to murder, a sacrilegious denial of God's image.[16] The Pharisees claimed to be more religious than other Jews, and they asserted that their explanations of Jewish law were more precise.[17] By the time of Jesus' ministry, this pride, this lack of humility, had become contagious among the Pharisees. No wonder Jesus called them hypocrites:

> But woe to you, scribes and Pharisees, hypocrites! For you lock people out of the kingdom of heaven. For you do not go in yourselves, and when others are going in, you stop them....

> Woe to you, scribes and Pharisees, hypocrites! For you clean the outside of the cup and of the plate, but inside they are full of greed and self-indulgence. You blind Pharisee! First clean the inside of the cup, so that the outside also may become clean.

> Woe to you, scribes and Pharisees, hypocrites! For you are like whitewashed tombs, which on the outside look beautiful, but inside they are full of the bones of the dead and of all kinds of filth. So you also on the outside look righteous to others, but inside you are full of hypocrisy and lawlessness.[18]

Humility, Agape

Hence the admonition is to maintain humility! To be religious, a person must have discovered humility. The only way this can be done is with self-examination, criticism, and love.[19]

In dialogues with Paul Tillich,[20] Professor Brown and a Franciscan father pointed out that a major problem in monastic life is the issue of pride—self-love. The issue also comes up in the lives of the saints. All too often, as young professionals become more virtuous, more faithful, and more understanding, the element of pride keeps emerging to negate all they think they have done. These professionals separated self-love from self-affirmation and the courage to be one's self.

Tillich said one solution is in the principle of forgiveness and acceptance of the unacceptable. He defined *agape* as "that form of love in which God loves us in spite of our imperfections, and in which we are to love our neighbor, especially if we do not like him."[21] It is also the form of love where we love ourselves despite our mistakes and imperfections. Constant awareness of our shortcomings helps maintain our humility.

I believe there are two other solutions: compassion and sympathy—identification with the one who is hurting. This is the Buddhist's approach. One of the most effective ways to maintain compassion and avoid belligerence is to be self-critical. One cannot always assume one's actions are on God's side. They need to be examined. Jewish prophet Amos saw the Lord using Assyria as his instrument to punish the people of Israel for their own violence. Jesus said, "First take the log out of your own eye, and then you will see clearly to take the speck out of your brother's eye."[22]

Only by acknowledging our own pain and suffering are we able to empathize with others. What are our enemies' perceived injustices? The Greeks put human misery on stage in their tragedies. The chorus regularly instructed the audience to weep for those whose concerns would normally fill them with abhorrence. Tragedy cannot be denied. It has to be brought into our midst and made a force for compassion. At the end of *The Iliad* Achilles and Priam wept together. As they shared their grief and saw each other as a mirror image, they recovered the humanity they lost in war. Karen Armstrong said that we have to be self-conscious and aware, and to see the others in our pain. Tragedy and The Golden Rule must extend our compassion to every person in the world. Empathy and compassion do not just sound edifying; they actually work.[23]

Perhaps it was recognizing the danger of self-pride that led to Hindu and Buddhist gurus, guides for deeper relationships with the Eternal. Both Hinduism and Buddhism sought additional ways to go behind or beyond their gods to that Ultimate Unity, including the unity of all opposites, even unity of good and evil. The guru filled a niche for many between daily living and the gods. The Hindu god Shiva is depicted with a great deal of symbolism. Dancing with one foot in the air, the other on the back of a dwarf, represents holding down his own ego. Dancing and enjoying himself, he is shown encircled by flame. Touch the ground as Buddha did, proving to yourself that you are here, a part of the world. As such, you are entitled to play a role, including enjoying yourself. Do so with full awareness of yourself, and without an attitude of superiority.

Self-love

Self-love is clearly necessary. Without self-love, one becomes egocentric—selfish. Disgust towards oneself is the same thing.[22] Without self-love, one feels empty and searches continuously, but aimlessly, for some diversion of momentary pleasure: sex, drugs, the excitement of criminal acts. These leave one still feeling meaningless-emptiness. He/she is also apt to feel anger. Negative attention is preferable to being ignored. A person can always get negative attention by being delinquent or acting out—even sexually—to get attention.

Alienation from one's self may be displaced to another person as hostility. This results in acts of cruelty, mayhem, or murder. If not displaced, alienation may cause thoughts of suicide. If there is no discernable pathway to a better life with fulfilling love, then there is no hope. Without hope, the thoughts of suicide may well be put into action. Paul Tillich expressed the same concepts. "Emptiness drives the human mind to strong reactions, and if they are not creatively good, they may become evil indeed."[23] Without self-love, love of others is impossible.

Self-esteem

A major part of self-love is self-esteem. Self-esteem rests on four pillars:

1. Feeling Worthy

The first of these is *feeling worthy* of being loved, which is developed from three sources. The most important foundation for a sense of lovability is the message of being loved by one's parents. If you experience their love as an infant and as a child, you feel lovable. If you experience their derision, neglect, or abuse (verbal or physical), your sense of lovability is significantly impaired.

The second confirmation of one's worth comes from close friends, from sweethearts as a teen, from lovers, and from one's spouse. The more esteem and love you have for them, the more their affection for you makes you feel lovable. This is the main reason romantic rejection hurts so much.

The third major message of worthiness comes from the community in the form of acceptance, respect, and recognition. From experiencing these loves, it follows naturally that God would love you, also. This sense of worthiness is addressed and reinforced by religion. "You are a child of God." "You are made in God's image." (See scripture quoted earlier.)

2. Being Capable

The second pillar of self-esteem is *capability*—one's abilities, skills, and knowledge—both intellectual and physical. A critical period for this development is ages 6–12. Children need to be supported as they explore new activities. The developmental issue is industry versus inferiority.[24] *I have something I can contribute.* In many households it begins with age-appropriate tasks and responsibilities. It also includes the parental teaching of compassion, helpfulness, honesty, and fairness. As the child matures, these traits mature, too. This form of spirituality is also found in the kindness and helpfulness of aboriginal people in dealing with strangers from the outside world.

It appears to be universal—a natural law. One gets a sense of achievement and adequacy from living such a life in feelings, thoughts, and actions. "I can do this on my own. I don't need a parental figure (or the church or God) reminding me what is the right way to think and behave." It is ingrained—written in one's mind and heart, as Brueggemann described.

3. Receiving Recognition

The third pillar of self-esteem is *receiving recognition* and esteem from others, peers, and respected members of the community. It is awareness of one's reputation and respect from others. This recognition merges with being identified as part of the community. The community nurtures its members; it guides and reinforces the development of ethics and morals. It also fosters and supports simple rituals of apology, forgiveness, and reconciliation. People are affirmed, confirmed, loved, and empowered. All of these aspects contribute to self-respect and generate confidence.

As this sense grows and the community expands in benevolence, in sensitivity and devotion, one feels a part of something greater than the self. In the United States the most common groupings of individuals into spirited communities are religious institutions. These are where individuals gather to share with each other, to enhance their spirituality, to be part of a group, and to feel, think, and act together in love of others. This, too, enhances self-esteem.

4. Evaluating Positively

The fourth pillar of self-esteem comes from *positive judgment* on how one is living his/her life after deep and significant reflection. "Am I on the path I want to be on?" This honest evaluation is absent from many people's lives. The Jews have institutionalized such reflection as part of Rosh Hashanah. Self-reflection is also important in Shinto; the most important of its three major symbols is the mirror. The other two are the sword and the jewel.[25] Negative judgment lowers self-esteem and engenders alienation. In the absence of reflection, people all too often cling to old evaluations that were self-given, or given earlier in life by someone they respected, perhaps a parent or teacher. One who believes he has lived up to his ideals in feelings, thoughts, and actions will experience an increase of self-esteem, confidence, and sometimes even spirituality. This is called achieving one's ego ideal.

Religion Seeks Social Justice

All the world's major religions have moved toward recognizing the value of each person, which in turn has led to greater emphasis on social justice. No longer fodder for the fates, every man, woman, and child has the capacity to find one's own connection to the Divine.

Recognition of the Divine within ourselves opens us to our need for self-love. As much as we discover that our self-love is reinforced by others, we also discover our own limitless capacity to love others. Only by loving others as much as we love ourselves are we ready to demand social justice for all.

Even though some use religion to corrupt our love of fellow man, religion teaches us all to live in peace. Just as the human mind seeks to integrate all its facets into a coherent whole, religion expresses our greatest endeavor: integrating all the people of the world into a coherent whole where all live in harmony.

NOTES FOR CHAPTER ELEVEN

11.1   *Bible*: 1 John 4:21

11.2   *Bible*: Matthew 25:40

11.3   See Chapter Four, "The Axial Age: New Prescription for Action"

11.4   *Bible*: Amos 3:1-2, Isaiah, Jeremiah, & Hosea

11.5   *Bible*: Jeremiah 31:33-34

11.6   Brueggemann, Walter: *A Social Reading of the Old Testament*, Fortress Press, Minneapolis, 1994, p. 48

11.7   Brueggemann: p. 48-49

11.8   *Bible*: Matthew 7:15-20

11.9   Wuthnow, Robert: *After Heaven, Spirituality in America Since 1950*, University of California Press, Berkley & Los Angeles, 1998, p. 170

11.10 *Bible*: Proverbs 14:31

11.11 *Bible*: Psalms 82:6

11.12 Hindery, Roderick: *Comparative Ethics in Hindu and Buddhist Traditions,* Motilal Banarsidass, Delhi, 1978, p. 46, 61-62

11.13 *Bible*: Luke 17:20-21

11.14 *Encyclopaedia Britannica*, 15th Ed, Vol 9, Encyclopaedia Britannica, Inc., p. 355

11.15 Armstrong, Karen: *The History of God*, Alfred A. Knopf, New York, 1993, p. 72

11.16 Armstrong: p. 78

11.17 Durant, Will: *The Story of Civilization, Vol 3, Caesar and Christ*, Simon and Schuster, New York, 1944, p. 336

11.18 *Bible*: Matthew 23:13-29

11.19 Schleiermacher, Friedrich: *On Religion: Addresses in Response to its Cultured Critics*, Tice, Terrence N., trans., Knox Press, Richmond, VA, 1969, p. 121

11.20   Brown, D. MacKenzie: *Ultimate Concern, Tillich in Dialogues*, Harper and Row, New York City, 1965, p. 207

11.21   Brown: p. 197

11.22   Armstrong: *The Great Transformation*, p. 394

11.23   Armstrong: *The Great Transformation*, p. 387

11.24   Fromm, Erich: cited by Tillich in Brown, D. MacKenzie: *Ultimate Concern*, p. 48 & 206

11.25   Brown: p. 180-181

11.26   Erickson, Erick: *Childhood and Society*, Norton Co.

11.27   Parrinder, Geoffrey: *World Religions*, Facts on File Publications, New York City, New York, 1984, p. 363

CHAPTER TWELVE

Putting It All Together

By the late 1960s and early '70s, many major mainline American churches were in serious decline. A number of urban churches in decaying neighborhoods were in danger of being closed—sold or abandoned. In his book *Urban Churches; Vital Signs, Beyond Charity Toward Justice,*[1] Nile Harper details how 28 urban churches turned themselves around.

Consider three examples. The Windsor Village United Methodist Church of Houston, Texas, had 25 members when they began their turnaround. In seventeen years their membership had grown to 10,000.[2] The West Angeles Church of God in Christ of South Central Los Angeles grew from fifty members in 1969 to 15,000 by 1997.[3] The Palestine Mission Church of Kansas City grew from eleven members in 1959 to more than 3,000 by 1990.[4] What approaches helped these churches succeed?

Meet Community Needs

These churches excelled in meeting local people's needs—emotional, practical, and religious. They provided meaningful triggers for feelings of reverence, spirituality, and closeness to God. Their preaching addressed existential questions. They developed goal-oriented visions for the church and community, as well as plans to achieve them. These social-action plans benefited the churches, their neighborhoods, and the community. Parishioners felt enriched by being a part of their church communities. The churches did not narrow down, or become more rigid and controlling; rather, they became more inclusive. They expanded their circle of love, and everyone experienced it.

Introduce New Ministers

In every case, the turnaround process began with a new minister who exemplified personal authority and outstanding leadership. The major motivating force in each church was its deeply spiritual and creative worship service. Central to this service was preaching. In all cases, the scripture-based preaching was delivered with energy and power. The selected scriptures stressed God's unlimited love, salvation, and social-justice issues. These social issues were neither abstract nor about some distant community, but were those faced by members of the church and community every day. Harper described preaching at the

Olivet Institutional Baptist Church of Cleveland: "Dr. Moss has emphasized preaching that touches the spirit, inspires commitment, engages the mind, and moves believers to action. His preaching nurtures worshipers intellectually and spiritually. It is faith seeking understanding in order to act constructively. An invitation to follow Christ and to make a faith commitment comes right after the sermon…."[5]

Encourage Participation in Services

The worship services for these churches were culturally diverse and participatory in style. People came together to listen to the Word of God, sing, pray, praise, give thanks to God, forgive others and the self, bring offerings, celebrate the sacraments, and affirm one another in Christ. The praise and giving of thanks to God has the effect of countering the attitudes of victimization, suffering, and hopelessness. Church members experienced respect, acceptance, affirmation, and encouragement. The spirit of love, like all emotions, is contagious. The churches became places of joy and laughter. Members' self-esteem grew. They bonded with others. The churches held multiple services at a variety of times on Sundays and during the week. Services were often tailored to various groups within the congregations, such as teens and young adults. This variation was especially evident in the music programs. Each church had a rich and expanded music program, including a number of choirs, musicians, and song and worship leaders.

Focus on the Community

The leaders of the churches stressed that the second most important attribute for success, after the worship service, was focusing on benefits for the community. "There is no substitute for a big vision of social justice that is challenging and compelling enough to win support of the congregation and the participation of those who can make it happen, including people outside of the congregation." To this end, the churches expanded their governing bodies to engage skilled people from the wider community, and to acquire specific talents. This wide collaboration strengthened everyone's commitment and dedication.[6] Many of these visions involved long-term projects. Even in the thinking and talking stages, these efforts widely signaled that "This church is on the move." "Action, social justice, will be increased to match our words and our expanded spirit." These visions focused on love for others and involvement of the "entire congregation" in the proposed action. Thus, a feedback loop was created, which increased self-esteem and love. In addition, they grew a sense of achievement and the realization of helping others. Members enjoyed strong feelings of camaraderie with other church members, of belonging and of being part of something greater than the self.

Move Toward Inclusivity

Most of these churches also moved to become more inclusive. At Mt. Auburn Presbyterian Church of Cincinnati they first addressed this issue in their theology. As a result, they opened their Holy Communion to all people who were present when the Lord's Supper was celebrated. "Everyone is welcome to participate: baptized or not, Christian or not, adult or child." This meant everyone was entitled to receive the richness of God's unbounded love. Jesus would eat with anyone. He would not have turned anyone away.[7] They also changed their profession of faith from a thought statement, "Do you take Jesus as your savior?", to an action statement, "Will you serve God as revealed in the life and ministry of Jesus?" They put their belief in God's love for everyone into practice by accepting all people, by becoming a welcoming congregation—expanding their circle. "…We affirm that gay and lesbian persons are part of God's good creation and that they, no less than heterosexual persons, are meant to enjoy God's gifts of love, joy and intimacy. All who seek and receive God's love are welcome as full participants in the life and worship of Christ's church without having to deny or hide their sexual orientation…" They clearly understood their policy would be perceived by the denomination as ecclesiastical disobedience, but they remained steadfast in their new position. They expanded their circle of love to be fully inclusive.

Commit to Social Justice Projects

These churches did not just attack "simple problems." Rather, they tackled projects demanding commitment to social justice. They addressed problems their members and the community were struggling with each day, such as affordable housing, education, health care, economic development, addiction, street crime, gang activity, and neighborhood blight. Several churches sponsored AA programs and attacked gang activities with the same general approach. Each addict or gang member had a sponsor who was available at all times, 24/7. The unconditional love of God—manifest in the respect, caring, and love of the sponsor—is the primary lever enabling them to move beyond the drugs or gang culture. This relationship with community members was called "the body of Christ," the extension of the incarnation that becomes the transforming and improving community.

Some churches purchased "crack houses" and deserted or dilapidated buildings in their immediate neighborhoods, then remodeled and sold or rented them at affordable rates. In some cases, they would repair the buildings, paying union wages, and use them for activity space and other programs (e.g.: tutoring, night shelter). Often, construction employers were expected to hire church members for some of the work, thus creating employment to support congregant families. Some churches then created a management company. Often a church would use income from one property as leverage to buy another. This process also created good jobs that put community people to work, thus enhancing economic development. In this way, the areas around the churches became increasingly safe.

The Olivet Institutional Baptist Church of Cleveland built a multi-million dollar holistic healthcare center, which was staffed by medical doctors, psychologists, clergy, and other professionals working in collaboration with the Cleveland Clinic and Western Reserve University. Stressing prevention and education, they addressed many areas, including loving relationships with one's mate; interpersonal communication skills; parenting skills; prayer, faith, belief, and healing; weight control; meditation and relaxation skills; and laughter as preventative medicine.

In 1992 The New Song Community Church of Baltimore, in partnership with Habitat for Humanity, began to implement its vision of rehabilitating 100 homes in a twelve-block area of the church within five years. By the summer of 1997, only 75 units had been completed and were owner occupied. A construction blitz in the summer and fall of that year completed the remaining 25 homes.[8] In this project, the church developed apprentice programs through which people learned carpentry, plumbing, electrical, and masonry skills, plus earned union certification.

The Mt. Auburn Presbyterian Church of Cincinnati invited various groups to use office space in the church. These included the Nuclear Freeze Campaign; the League of Women Voters; Amnesty International; the Center for Peace Education; the American Civil Liberties Union; the University of Cincinnati Child Care Center; Women's City Club; social-justice advocacy groups; Physicians for Social Responsibility; Parents and Friends of Lesbians and Gays; the Family Care Network; Cincinnati Youth Group (for teenage lesbians and gays); and Ecumenical Campus Ministries. The groups paid modest rental fees, which were invested in program expansion, building improvements, and maintenance. The interaction between the congregation and civic groups benefited both. The church grew in membership and social commitment while the organizations gained active supporters from the congregation.

Offer Social Services

Many churches established soup kitchens and food pantries. Some offered meals, perhaps just before Sunday school. Others offered regular meals several days a week. A number of churches provided space and secretarial staff for medical clinics in cooperation with hospitals and other medical centers. Night-time child care was offered in many communities with night-shift workers. Some churches offered night shelter and care for abandoned and abused women, and social-services referral services.

Develop Self-improvement Programs

Although each church embraced numerous projects, none became involved with all of the projects mentioned. Participation in every project was open to the public. There were singles groups, classes on marriage—with counseling, if needed—parenting, cooking, money management, meditation, relaxation, exercise, and study skills. Some churches had preschool and after-school programs with alternative activities for teens, including dance, art, drama, writing, computers, gymnastics, and basketball. Tutoring and mentoring programs were common, and some churches established learning centers.

Some churches organized to improve education in partnership with public schools. Other churches opened alternative schools. These schools emphasized honesty, cooperation, responsibility, respect for others, hard work, self-discipline, and pursuit of excellence. They insisted on parental involvement, and followed up by teaching parents how to help their children learn. They trained in non-violent street survival skills and conflict resolution. Youths also participated in field trips to interesting places, which presented new possibilities for their lives.

Working in partnership with public institutions, some churches offered adult literacy programs and coaching for GED. They provided pre-job and on-the-job training, attitudinal training, employment referrals, and follow-up. Some even helped groups of members establish businesses. A greeting card company run by teens was one example. The New Song Community Church of Baltimore created "Sandtown Records," which records and sells music CDs, and sponsors a children's choir recording group.[9] Churches operated restaurants, ran bakeries and catering services, managed real estate, operated credit unions, and brokered home repairs. These activities developed community life, put people to work, and promoted social justice.

Address Local Issues

Some churches tackled social-justice issues such as adequate trash pickup and police protection. One addressed the way contractors and others dealt with the day-labor pool. Some employers were charging for transportation to the job, and for equipment such as hard hats. Some workers were paid only in scrip, redeemable only at certain stores, often only at liquor stores. Churches in Atlanta collaborated to gain a city ordinance to make these practices illegal, and to set fair labor standards.

In run-down communities, the churches were in a unique position to offer credible commitments which few individuals and other institutions could match. The churches had the trust of institutions they were dealing with, offering integrity, stability, and the staying power to see projects through. These projects gave the participants an increase of self-esteem and basic dignity. The sharing and caring created a sense of belonging, both to the church and to the community. Each person was part of something greater than the self.

Put It All Together

People thrive where they are accepted, respected, and able to contribute; where they have realistic opportunity and hope for a positive future.[10] These churches put it all together. They offered positive feelings to counter thoughts of suffering, victimization, and unworthiness, as well as depression and lack of hope for improvement. The thought aspect is exemplified by the vision with all its subparts and projects. Thought was focused on the self-development of people, on helping others and making the community a better place to live. The sermons and worship services also stressed existential questions of salvation—including the afterlife—and the questions of "How am I to relate to others?" Consideration of these questions gave affirmation and meaning to life. The demand made by membership was a demand to be a part—to contribute money, time, energy, and talent to the vision of the church. All of this resulted in the ongoing realization, "I am a part of all of this, and it is good."

These social actions meet Wuthnow's standard for Action Oriented Spirituality. They go beyond those advocated by the mainline liberal churches. By giving members realistic pride, these actions enabled individuals to live their ego ideals, which raises self-esteem. Their circle of inclusion had been expanded from immediate family to the community, or "The world becomes our parish, not just the neighborhood."

With all of these elements in place, is it any wonder that people of all races and all walks of life flock to these churches?

NOTES FOR CHAPTER TWELVE

12.1   Harper, Nile and associates: *Urban Churches, Vital Signs: Beyond Charity Toward Justice*, William B. Eerdmans Publishing Company, Grand Rapids, Michigan; Cambridge, U.K., 1999

12.2   Harper: p. 223

12.3   Harper: p. 254

12.4   Harper: p. 1193 & 195

12.5   Harper: p. 115

12.6   Harper: p. 116

12.7   Harper: p. 129

12.8   Harper: p. 115

12.9   Harper: p. 17

12.10 Harper: p. 255

CHAPTER THIRTEEN

Peace and Diversity

The Divine is present in all religions. Religious reverence is the glorious experience of our relationship to the whole—the Holy. Many different finite situations and objects can trigger religious feelings and awareness of the Infinite. Throughout history, every culture has expressed its encounter with the Infinite differently.[1] Paul Tillich notes that Jesus as described in the biblical book of Mark is different from how he is described by the other gospels of the *Bible*.[2] In the first three centuries after Christ, Christianity had at least a hundred major differences in beliefs, plus many more minor variations.[3] Christianity might have developed into multiple religions had Constantine not called the council at Nicea and forced a unified doctrine. Christianity as an umbrella term for multiple religions, each with slightly different icons and concepts, would be how Hinduism is today. Each church or individual would celebrate his/her own quasi-individual creed, all recognized as sacred, possibly even accepted, not merely tolerated.

More Than Tolerance, Acceptance

One of the oldest proclamations in favor of religious freedom was set forth in 1568 by King John Sigismund Zapolya of Transylvania: "…in every place the preachers shall preach and explain the Gospel each according to his understanding of it, and if the congregation like it, well, if not, no one shall compel them for their souls would not be satisfied, but they shall be permitted to keep a preacher whose teaching they approve….no one shall be reviled for his religion by anyone,…and it is not permitted that anyone should threaten anyone else by imprisonment or by removal from his post for his teaching…"[4]

An important step toward acceptance is acknowledging that concepts of God do vary. In Judaism some early rabbis promoted this idea. They tended to avoid constructing any formal doctrines about God; instead, they treated God as an almost tangible presence among the people. They considered this presence so strong that any general doctrine would seem inappropriate. In their view, God adapts his presence to the ability of each person to receive Him. God could not be defined exactly the same way for everyone. To this day, theological ideas about God are officially private matters in much of Judaism. However, there are numerous theological traditions for describing God in Judaism, which is also true within Protestantism and Catholicism. It might seem then that any explicitly demanded official doctrine would limit the essential mystery of God.[5]

In the early centuries of Christianity, judgment about other religions was determined by the idea of the Logos. Church fathers emphasized the universal presence of the Logos, the Word.[6] The Logos is present everywhere. In this light, in the 5th century Augustine would say that true religion had existed always, but it was called Christianity only after the appearance of Christ. Christianity did not consider itself to be so much an exclusive religion as an all-inclusive religion.[7]

Christians need to be ever-mindful that Jesus never claimed to be the only messenger from God. Remember, every particular religion has limited horizons. No one is capable of embracing all forms of the Infinite.[8] Each person must be conscious that his religion is only part of a whole. The Infinite that one person sees in a different religion may be beyond another's horizon.[9] Countless people might feel religious, but each could have different markers to designate that feeling.[10] God is greater than any particular form in which his manifestations can occur.[11] Tillich also said, "Every period of human history expresses its encounter between the infinite in ourselves and the whole universe in different images. The uniqueness of every individual and every period makes it necessary that there be many religions."[12] The degree and depth of religious diversity within political boundaries will be grossly limited unless there is tolerance—or, better yet, acceptance of other people's religions.

Not only does each period in history encounter the world and the Ultimate differently, but each individual does so, too. Individuals might be at different places in their understandings, or they might be on different paths. The Hindus and Buddhists instituted the practice of having a personal guru for each seeker, not only to protect their adherents from too much pride, but to help them grow at a rate that was best for them. Tillich said it is necessary to have many religions, and that any struggle among religions is unnecessary.[13] The victory of one religion over all others would destroy in each the concreteness that gives it dynamic power.[14]

All religions have both a *mystical aspect* and an *ethical-cultish aspect*. The mystical experience is a feeling of closeness to the Divine. It is here and now. The ethical-cultish aspect is the ideal, the way things ought to be. This is also the *community aspect*, so it has its own unique variations on the symbols that represent a community's or a people's ideals. There is a tension between these two aspects. Various religions' denominations have varying degrees of these two aspects. Without both myth and cult (rituals) a religion would lose its revelatory experiences.[15]

Schleiermacher said the multiplicity of religions and the most distinct differences between them are both necessary and unavoidable.[16] He added that nothing is more irreligious than to demand religious uniformity among humanity.[17] Coercion is counter-productive in matters of religion.[18] In the *Qur'an*, Mohammad said, "Let there be no coercion in religious matters."[19]

This approach calls for acceptance of differences—not mere tolerance, but full acceptance. This admonition also applies to religious differences. In learning to accept, the following statements should be kept in mind: You can't necessarily expect to see the Infinite in the same finite expressions that are holy to another person. Further, others may not be able to examine your finite ways or objects and find transparency to the Infinite in the same way you hold so dear. We need to acknowledge that others' views of the Eternal may be different from our own, but if theirs are based on love, they may be just as valid as our own.

Of course, this does not mean that there can be no understandings of God that are held in common in a faith community, or a nation, or even the world. Those who have learned to discern the Eternal have often been quiet souls. Either they are alone with themselves and the Infinite, or when they look about them, they gladly allow anyone to pursue his own way. Discerning the Eternal brings understanding that there is a wide path for humans toward actualizing love and relating to the Infinite.[20]

Criteria for Interfaith Dialogue

Productive interfaith dialogue depends on agreeing to some basic criteria for respectful discussion. All parties need to acknowledge the value of each regarding their own and others' religious convictions. We can assume that each party is able to represent his own religious convictions. All must have a common desire to understand and compare concepts. Each needs to be open to criticism directed against his/her own religious basis.[21] Further, there should be no attempt to proselytize in the settings in which the dialogue takes place.

There is no cause for religious intolerance except to protect someone's vested interests. Even temple priests, clergy, entire religious denominations, and secular politicians may commit acts of intolerance. Such action may be motivated by the desire for political power, or to gain support in times of conflict, including war. Mr. Dawud Walid, Executive Director of the Council on American-Islamic Relations of Michigan said, "If the Jews lived up to the spirit of their own sacred texts, and if the Christians lived up to the spirit of their sacred texts, and if the Muslims lived up to the spirit of their sacred texts, there would be no war between them."

The Goal of All Religions Is Love

Love, compassion, empathy, and The Golden Rule will do much to eliminate interpersonal conflict. For there to be peace among communities or nations, there must be social justice, which includes rapid and fair resolution of conflict. No one is to be regarded as above or below another person in the religious realm. The Dalai Lama has said, "...the goal of all religions is love." To the question, "Which is the greatest commandment in the law?" Jesus replied,

> You shall love the Lord your God with all your heart, and with all your soul, and with all your mind. This is the greatest and first commandment. And the second is like it: 'You shall love your neighbor as yourself.' [22]

These are the same differences between mystical and ethical-cult discussed earlier. One relates us to the Divine, the other to fellow humans. Love is the most powerful and important aspect of religion. Love overcomes separateness and brings us into communion with the Ultimate.

How Large Is Your Circle of Love?

The critical question is, Who is inside your inner circle of love? We regard the people within our circle as worthy of our love. The people in our circle are those we wish to be loved by. Many people have concentric circles, one outside of another. Is your largest circle only for those who believe as you do?—your cult, your nation, your ethnicity, your religion? It is relatively easy to love humanity in the abstract, but much more difficult to love everyone with whom we have contact. How is your love put into actions? How large is your circle of genuine concern—love—for your fellow humans?

In the 16th century, Francis David, a Unitarian minister, grasped the truth that this book seeks to illuminate.[23] He authored a saying that has become a commonly used Unitarian Universalist adage:

"We don't have to think alike to love alike."[24]

NOTES FOR CHAPTER THIRTEEN

13.1   Tillich, Paul: *A History of Christian Thought*, A Touchstone Book, Simon & Schuster, New York City, 1967, p. 397

13.2   Brown, D. MacKenzie: *Ultimate Concern, Tillich in Dialogues*, Harper and Row, New York City, 1965, p.154

13.3   Durant, Will: *The Story of Civilization, Vol 3, Caesar and Christ*, Simon and Schuster, New York, 1944, p. 604-5

13.4   Parke, David: *The Epic of Unitarianism: Original Writings from the History of Liberal Religion*, Skinner House Books, Boston, 1986, p. 19

13.5   Armstrong, Karen: *A History of God*, A Borzoi Book, Alfred A. Knopf, New York, 1993, p. 73-4

13.6   *Bible*: See preface to the book of John

13.7   Tillich, Paul: *Christianity and the Encounter of World Religions*, Columbia University Press, NYC, 1961, p. 34-5

13.8   Schleiermacher, Friedrich: *On Religion: Addresses in Response to its Cultured Critics*, Tice, Terrence N., trans., Knox Press, Richmond, VA,1969, p. 99

13.9   Schleiermacher: p. 100

13.10   Schleiermacher: p. 98

13.11   Tillich: *A History of Christian Thought*, p. 146

13.12   Tillich: p. 397

13.13   Tillich: p. 397, 375 & 399

13.14   Tillich: *Christianity and the Encounter of World Religions*, p. 96

13.15   Tillich: p. 58 & 93

13.16   Schleiermacher: p.274

13.17   Schleiermacher: p. 321

13.18   Armstrong, Karen: *The Battle for God*, Ballantine Publishing Group, New York, 2001, p. 16

13.19   *Qur'an*: "*The Meaning of the Qur'an*", Ali, Abdullah Yusuf, trans., Al-Attique Pub., Surah 2: 256

13.20   Schleiermacher: p. 101 (partially paraphrased)

13.21   Tillich: p. 62

13.22   *Bible*: Matthew 22:34

13.23   Brown: p. 3

13.24   Personal Communication from Unitarian Universalist Home Office: www.info@uua.org

CHAPTER FOURTEEN

Harmony

Religion infuses many of our most powerful *feelings*. It occupies our *thoughts* as we seek understanding and decide how it will shape our lives. It drives many of our *actions*, both in how we practice our faith and how we conduct our affairs with others. Harmony is the *feeling* we all desire, the goal we can and should *think* about how to pursue, and the great potential result of our most worthy *actions*. In our quest for harmony within ourselves and among others, we must actively strive to achieve worldwide acceptance of all religions—not mere tolerance, but full acceptance.

We must recognize that religious feelings throughout history have been, and continue to be, the same in every religion, even though the founders may have followed unique paths in discovering transcendence to the Divine. Central to religion are the core feelings of piety and love. Buddah called these feelings compassion. Mohammad called them mercy—mercy from God and mercy to and from others. Rooted in these feelings are our codes of ethics, which guide our thoughts and actions. The ethics of all religions advocate charity, forgiveness, social justice, and treating others as we would have them treat us. While the details might vary, we should appreciate that all religions address the essential issues of life, and all urge us to honor others.

Neuroscience confirms how we all process information in very similar ways. The right side of the human brain usually deals with intuition and feelings, evaluating situations with a holistic approach. The left side approaches information analytically. The focused interaction of these halves can result in religious awe, the loss of sense of self, a feeling of merging with the world and/or God, the *Uno Mysterica*. The physiology of achieving this transcendence is the same regardless of whichever religion we choose to guide our beliefs and practices.

We are all curious, inquisitive, logical, and intuitive. We need to fill in the gaps in our understanding. This process of *confabulation* may lead to variations in religious symbols, forms of worship, creeds, and doctrines. It is a process that continues with newly discovered concepts and messages, even though religions' sacred scriptures tend to remain the same. We can appreciate the benefits of having so many different versions of religion if we accept that they merely represent different and sometimes evolving expressions of our common core values.

Although the basic values remain true over time, how members practice their religions evolve over time. As the world changes, societies adapt. Their symbols, including religious symbols, are finite, bound to their culture. The most effective religious symbols are recognized as transparent to the Ultimate. When a religious symbol or concept begins to lose its helpfulness, then change is inevitable. Changes may be minor or profound; they may be adopted quickly or may require up to hundreds of years to be accepted. The test of an effective concept or symbol is: Does the Infinite shine through? Today and moving forward, religions and their symbols must adapt to a changing world where people of all religions increasingly interact day to day. The danger of hostility grows ever more stark, while the benefits have never been greater if we find new ways to honor core values while seeking harmony among those who believe differently.

We all need self-love. Alienation from one's self may be displaced to another, resulting in acts of cruelty and worse. We cannot love others unless we love ourselves. Each of us must see our love for others as a worthy gift. If we cannot find it in ourselves to love one another, to embrace our common values and celebrate our differences, then our religions must adapt to help us discover the self-love from which harmony among all people grows and thrives.

The Divine is greater than any particular manifestation or concept. The Divine is present in all religions even though their concepts of God vary. People may be at different places in their understanding of God and religion. Even among the strict adherents of any particular religion there are vast differences in what people truly understand and believe, especially in how they draw upon their feelings for religious thoughts and actions. Appreciating the differences between people within our own religions helps us realize the value in appreciating people of other religions. The wide range of mystical and ethical aspects from one religion to another, from one congregation to another, or even one individual to another offers a rich and exciting opportunity to learn and grow and appreciate.

We need respectful dialogues among members of various religions to increase understanding. We are not each other's enemies. All religions espouse love, justice, compassion, and mercy.

We must strive to sustain the best of what our religions offer. We must adapt our thinking, and teach each new generation the value of acceptance.

We must widen our circle of concern for humanity in the wondrous quest for harmony among all people.

We begin by asking ourselves the question I pose for each of you:

How big is *your* circle of concern?

Acknowledgments

I am indebted to many people for their help and assistance with this book. They are all very caring, compassionate people. Most of them have become friends in the process.

Terry Tice, PhD

First and foremost among these is my long-term friend, Dr. Terry Tice, who holds doctorates in theology from Princeton University and in philosophy from the University of Michigan. He has spent most of his professional life on the faculty at Michigan. Terry has created a legacy with his large number of articles and books, many of them translations of religious writings from German to English. Almost anywhere in the western world or the Middle East Terry can be received by former students with warm appreciation. He is always giving of his talents, his knowledge, and himself. When I first thought of using the distinctions among feeling, thinking, and acting 35 years before starting this book, Terry and I discussed how Friedrich Schleiermacher had written about these modalities but not used them as tools for comparing world religions. He encouraged me to explore the subject further, which I did in the decades since. Terry's insight and support proved invaluable for this project.

Nile Harper, PhD

Dr. Nile Harper holds a master's degree in religious education from Union Theological Seminary in NYC, and a doctorate in social foundations of education at Columbia University in NYC. Currently Director of Urban Church Research in Minneapolis, he has served in a wide range of positions from Professor of Sociology of Religion to campus pastor. His publications include *Social Conflict and Adult Christian Education; Will the Church Lose the City?* (with Kendig Cully); *Urban Churches, Vital Signs: Beyond Charity Toward Justice;* and *Journeys Into Justice.* Nile was one of the first people to read an early draft of this manuscript. He made numerous suggestions and bluntly pointed out where we disagreed, always offering reasons and references. He provided much of the material I examined in the chapter about successful urban churches. A dedicated friend whose contributions proved invaluable, Nile has earned the appreciation of both my mind and heart.

George B. Lambrides, MA

Rev. George B. Lambrides earned degrees in education and religion at Houghton College in New York and Denver Seminary in Colorado, then followed with another master's in counseling psychology in Oregon. He was the senior minister of the First Baptist Church in Ann Arbor, and served as Protestant chaplain at the University of Michigan for ten years. His career spanning religious and healthcare work includes founding the Interfaith Round Table in Washtenaw County, Michigan, and serving as co-executive Director with Susan King for nineteen years. George has proved to be an extremely valuable advisor, a source for many contacts, and a friend who introduced me to clergy of many different faiths.

Kenneth Phifer, PhD

Rev. Phifer earned his undergraduate degree from Harvard, and his masters and doctorate degrees from the University of Chicago Divinity School. A minister in the emerging Unitarian Universalist church, Nile printed some of his insightful sermons, which were found quite valuable by some of my psychiatric patients. Dedicated to teaching, he helped me find meaning and spirituality for the first time in my life. I appreciate his helpful comments about this manuscript.

Clergy of Other World Religions

I have benefited greatly from the critiques and counsel of a number of different clergy representing Hinduism, Buddhism, Judaism, and Islam. I have always considered their advice carefully, but have not always followed it. Several suggested that I include additional material on their religion. I read everything that each suggested, but felt strongly that I needed to maintain some semblance of balance in my dealing with all religions. I greatly appreciate their readings of the manuscript and the kindness each showed me.

Thanks to Rabbi **Robert Dobrusin** of the Beth Israel Congregation for his Jewish perspective; **Munir Munshey** for his expertise in Islam; **Sharada Kumar**, Acharya of the Chinmaya Mission in Ann Arbor, for her help with the Hindu perspective; and **Haju Murray**, for sharing her Buddhist viewpoint.

Stephen Geez, MA

Stephen holds degrees in psychology and in English language & literature, plus a master's in education and community development, all from the University of Michigan. A novelist, non-fiction writer, educator, and publisher with Fresh

Ink Group, he has founded non-profit community-based organizations, plus developed televised and multi-media communications for major corporations. We have grown quite close working on this and other projects together. My long-term friend and editor, he has offered exhaustive input and advice from the earliest drafts through the final publication proposal, provided market and industry research, and oversaw publication.

Ann Stewart, managing director of The Fresh Ink Group, provided a wide range of management, from file preparation through developing industry contacts.

Patsy LaFave and **Beem Weeks** provided extensive word processing and file revisions with exacting excellence. Both showed tremendous patience and persistence in deciphering my handwritten notes, plus incorporating Stephen's and my innumerable rounds of revision.

Jonathon Gross, my son-in-law, spared me countless hours of frustration by tracking down references, sometimes based on little more than my telling him the essence of scriptures I wanted. His skills navigating the World Wide Web and his commitment to this project have proved invaluable.

Jane Sharpe, my sister, provided a careful reading, helpful comments, editorial suggestions, and welcome encouragement.

Marguerite (Peggy) Shearer, MD, always has been and continues to be supportive of all my endeavors. She is my wonderful wife of more than half a century.

About the Author

Marshall L. Shearer, MD

Marshall L. Shearer earned his doctor's degree from the Medical College of South Carolina in 1958. After a general rotating internship, he came to the University of Michigan for psychiatric training. While his wife, Marguerite, practiced family medicine, Marshall conducted research and certification in child psychiatry, and consulted on psychiatric evaluations for the Michigan Department of Corrections. The Shearers joined the Bushnell Congregational Church in Detroit. While Marshall taught Sunday School, both served as resource physicians for a church-sponsored sex-education program divided between junior- and senior-high students.

Once Marshall completed his psychiatric training, he joined the University of Michigan faculty full-time, first as Instructor, then as Assistant Professor. He became a diplomat of the American Board of Neurology and Psychiatry in Psychiatry, and later of the same Board in Child Psychiatry. As Assistant In-patient Director at the university's Children's Psychiatric Hospital, Marshall worked with ward staff and with parents regarding their hospitalized children. He consulted part-time for the Ann Arbor and Wayne-Westland public school systems.

The Board of Directors of the Reproductive Biological Research Foundation—later known as the Masters and Johnson Institute—recruited the Shearers as a couple widely skilled in the fields of psychiatry, medicine, and academia/ teaching. They spent two years at the Institute in St. Louis, Missouri, where Marshall's responsibilities included treating patients, developing a curriculum with Mrs. Johnson to train other professionals.

Religious training was integral to Marshall's upbringing; three lines of his family tree consisted of ministers about every other generation. His maternal grandfather was a Professor of Old Testament and Greek. His parents' plan to become missionaries was thwarted only by lack of funding. Family tragedy and a keen desire to resolve unsatisfactory explanations and nagging contradictions set Marshall on a path to seek spiritual understanding. Although by his teen years he considered himself atheist, his pursuit of religious insight has continued throughout his life. He participated in a study group for the world's great religions during graduate school. He eventually found a church and home in the First Unitarian Universalist Church where his contributions have included developing a formal youth-mentoring program. Marshall has long discussed and debated religious issues with author/translator and now-retired Professor of Theology Terry Tice, PhD, a former student of the great religious thinker Paul Tillich.

Marshall and Peggy wrote *Maximizing Happiness Through Intimate Communication*, a comprehensive self-help system for understanding and nurturing meaningful relationships, and launched www.DocShearer.com. They developed a companion workshop, then after two years turned it over to other professionals to expand, and wrote the book *Sex, Frankly*. Marshall continued his own research on religious issues, consulted with many experts in various world religions, and drafted *Toward Interfaith Harmony*, the unique melding of his career unlocking mysteries of the human mind and a personal quest seeking answers to how the world's peoples find meaning in their spiritual potential. He sought feedback from religious leaders of many faiths as he refined the text, during which he also published *My Life and Spiritual Journey*, a personal account of his own quest for knowledge. He devoted his retirement years largely to religious studies, hoping to continue the journey with ideas and feedback from readers of all faiths, as well as those with no faith at all. He passed away at home in 2014 after completing *Toward Interfaith Harmony*, which has been published in his honor posthumously.

Fresh Ink Group

Publishing
Free Memberships
Share & Read Free Stories, Essays, Articles
Free-Story Newsletter
Writing Contests

&

Books
E-books
Amazon Bookstore

&

Authors
Editors
Artists
Professionals
Publishing Services
Publisher Resources

&

Members' Websites
Members' Blogs
Social Media

FreshInkGroup.com
Email: info@FreshInkGroup.com
Twitter: @FreshInkGroup
Google+: Fresh Ink Group
Facebook.com/FreshInkGroup
LinkedIn: Fresh Ink Group
About.me/FreshInkGroup

Fresh Ink Group

Maximizing Happiness Through Intimate Communication
3rd Edition

Marshall L. Shearer, MD
Marguerite R. Shearer, MD

True love is nurtured in the conviction that you both value your partner's happiness as much as your own, but achieving such confidence in any relationship is a challenge, even for the most committed. No matter what lifestyle you pursue together, it's through honest communication that you will learn to protect yourselves and each other, to shed the encumbrances of clutter and noise as you propel your own unique Spiral of Love to exhilarating new heights.

From finding your soulmate through growing old together, *Maximizing Happiness Through Intimate Communication* lays out a complete system with everyday examples, simply explaining relationship dynamics like persistent problems, the transformation of hurts, concepts of time, components of anger, addictions, turning work into play, protecting vulnerability, reinforcing trust, sexual communication, and the neverending stages of love's spiral.

Don't be discouraged by media-packaged gimmicks and the one-size-fits-all advice from self-help gurus. Become the experts of your own relationship, and discover the best of growing yourselves that ultimate, most meaningful love.

FreshInkGroup.com

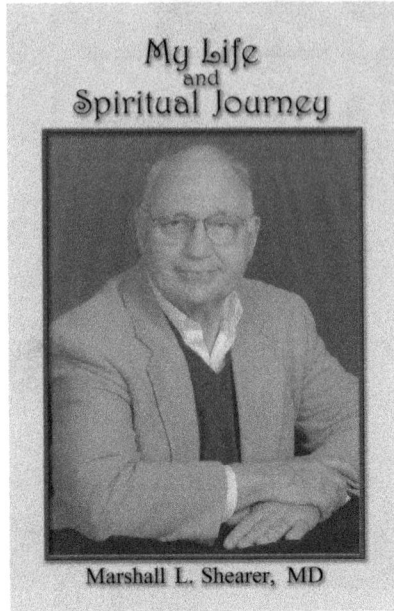

My Life
and
Spiritual Journey

Marshall L. Shearer, MD

The child of a military family, young Marshall Shearer dealt with personal trag-edy by formulating poignant questions that led to contradictory and unsatis-factory religion-based explanations. He never stopped seeking answers, even as he has enjoyed a wonderful life: medical school, loving marriage, beautiful family, and a distinguished career dedicated to helping people learn to live happily, to embrace others, and to cherish life. Through it all, he persisted as a student of the world's religions, asking new and ever-more sophisticated questions and finding answers we can all accept, from atheists to the most devout. Having developed his own unique perspective for understanding our place in the world, he continues to share his vision through books rang-ing from how to grow successful relationships to advocating bold new ways to achieve harmony among all religions. In *My Life and Spiritual Journey*, Dr. Shearer tells us his own story, the intimate perspective of one determined man who refuses to compromise in his quest to discover the acceptance we all seek and deserve.

FreshInkGroup.com

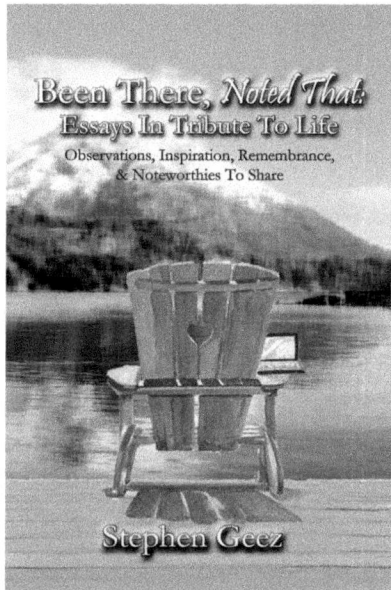

The simple lives of everyday people in a mundane world prove extraordinary in this collection of 54 personal-experience essays by novelist Stephen Geez. The eclectic mix of memoir, commentary, humor, and appreciation covers a wide range of topics, each beautifully illustrated by artists and photographers from the Fresh Ink Group. Geez catches what many of us miss, then considers how we might all share the most poignant of lessons. *Been There, Noted That* aims to reveal who we are, examine where we've been, and discover what we dare strive to become.

FreshInkGroup.com

www.ingramcontent.com/pod-product-compliance
Lightning Source LLC
Chambersburg PA
CBHW060858280326
41934CB00007B/1106